A Culinary Journey

IN

Gascony

Recipes and Stories from

My French Canal Boat

Kate Ratliffe

TEN SPEED PRESS

BERKELEY, CALIFORNIA

Ten Speed Press
Box 7123
Berkeley, California 94707

Cover and interior design by Big Fish Books, San Francisco
Food photography by Jonathan Chester
All other photographs by Kate Ratliffe

Library of Congress Cataloging-in-Publication Data
Ratliffe, Kate.
A culinary journey in Gascony; recipes and stories
from my french canal boat / Kate Ratliffe.
p.   cm.
Includes index.
ISBN 0-89815-753-6 (pbk.)
1. Cookery, French—Gascony style. 2. Garonne River Valley
(Spain and France)—Description and travel. I. Title.
TX719.2.G37R38   1995
641.59447'7—dc20   95-13465
                                        CIP

Printed in Hong Kong

1 2 3 4 5 6 7 8 9 10 — 99 98 97 96 95

This book is lovingly dedicated to three generations of Italian cooks: Petronella DiPietrantonio, who started the adventure by leaving an Abruzzi mountain village, Julia DiPietrantonio, who taught me to laugh and cook as she measured flour from her hand to mine, and my mother, Phyllis DiPietrantonio Hill, who in keeping alive her own adventures gave birth to mine. They traveled, cooked, worked, told stories, laughed, and, above all, encouraged the fourth generation's creative wanderlust.

The Canal Latéral à la Garonne

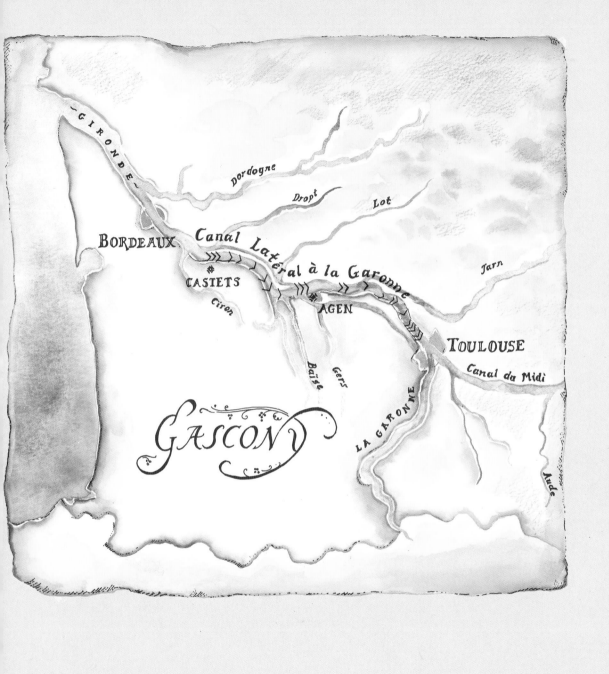

INTRODUCTION

ETWEEN CANAL'S END at Castets-en-Dorthe, where this book begins, and homeport at Ste. Colombe-en-Bruilhois, where we finish, there are over eighty-eight kilometers, twenty-one locks, and nineteen villages and towns lining a slow-moving canal in Southwest France. I call this my long village. The canal barge I live on is called the *Julia Hoyt*. She is eighty-five feet long, weighs sixty-five tons, and is nearly eighty years old. My husband, Patrick, and I sail the long village at a pace from another era. I slowly gather recipes and rituals from neighbors and friends, shopkeepers and lockkeepers. Since 1986, the *Julia Hoyt* has been my floating home, my one-table restaurant and two-room hotel. Long sunny days from spring until fall are filled with land-locked nautical activities as guests and friends are catered to and entertained. When winter approaches, the *Julia Hoyt* is retired for a few cold months. In the winter, I return to California to teach and write the recipes and tell the stories from the logbook of this historic Dutch barge afloat in Gascony.

For years, when friends would ask, "Where are you and the boat?" I would answer rather vaguely, "Somewhere in southwestern France." No one had ever heard of Castelnaudary, Agen, or Moissac. They thought that Toulouse was some artist's last name and Bordeaux was just a good red wine. But as I stayed from spring to spring and quit traveling the long river distances, "somewhere in southwestern France" became more and more specific. Just as I had fallen in love with big boats, barges, and canals, I had begun to fall in love with this Garonne River Valley, its own canal, and the people who refer to themselves and their cooking as Gascon. Not found on modern maps, the old province of Gascony is as much a gastronomical and cultural definition as it is geographical. Gascony is bordered by the Garonne River to the north and east, the Atlantic Ocean to the west, and the Pyrenees to the south.

The "big" town of Agen (population 40,000) became the gateway to my long village when Christian Barthe, barge builder and canal dreamer, became guardian angel to the *Julia Hoyt*. Christian was the first to teach me the meaning of Gascon hospitality. The weeks of travel up- and downstream on the Canal Latéral à la Garonne determined my April to November routines. The long village started to take its shape as I came to know the butcher in *that* village, the

The Julia Hoyt

baker over *there*, the markets in *these* towns, and the always-on-call mechanic just over the hill. Soon I had friends to visit in tiny Lagruère, two days' travel by boat or forty minutes by car. Or Patrick and I would call on Audrey and Tony on *Maja*, their converted Dutch barge, moored at Meilhan for the winter. Later, with friends, we would buy an old canal-side farm, Camont, to use as our homeport and anchor our wandering ways. The long village stretched, filled out, and became an epic poem of medieval names: Castets-en-Dorthe, La Reole, Fontet, Hure, Meilhan, Caumont, Fourgues, Pont des Sables, Marmande, Tonneins, Le Mas d'Agenais, Lagruère, St. Christoph, Damazan, Buzet, Bruch, Serignac, Brax, and Ste. Colombe-en-Bruilhois.

My long village is a string of villages and towns built 700 to 1,000 years ago. Most of the villages are no larger than 500 well-fed souls. They are evenly spaced along the canal, linked by the locks and sixty-eight bridges, each with a name, placed to slow you down and help you count the days. We pass slowly under tight-fitting stone arches scored by countless towropes, mile markers on the canal: Jean Serre, L'Auvignon, La Falotte, Pont des Sable. It takes a week of easy cruising at eight kilometers an hour to make this trip and visit the "neighbors," each in their own turn, day by day.

The first time I sailed this long village was during the spring. Plum trees were in full blossom, violet-tipped asparagus filled the farmers market stalls, grape-clustered wisteria draped across old stone porches like swooning ladies. The French soil was already well warmed by a determined sun and ready for the voluptuous landscapes promised in countless Impressionist paintings. So was I.

An unexpected April snow flurry skated down from the Pyrenees, halfheartedly dusting the canal-side gardens and pansy-filled window boxes. I thought I had escaped the northern climate of Holland, where I had found the *Julia Hoyt* and meandered the rivers and canals of inland Europe for six months, always turning south and heading for the southern sun. After the insistent rains of summer in 1987, a sunny October saw us leaving the flatlands and dikes of the Netherlands behind, a somber November reaching across the northern rivers of Belgium and France to cross the open fields near Reims as friends joined me to drink champagne in Champagne. December turned a sunny Provençal face to us as we battered the mistral down the Rhône River to Avignon. Lulled by the Mediterranean influences of the Midi, the *Julia Hoyt* and I passed the heart of winter with friends in Béziers before moving on to the last reach of the great Canal des Deux-Mers which flows toward Bordeaux and the Atlantic Ocean.

Now it was spring and I was still chasing the sun as the *Julia Hoyt* pivoted west on an old stone bollard at the Port de l'Embouchure in Toulouse. The windy Canal du Midi was left behind as the Canal Latéral carried us away from city and industry at every six-foot-deep lock. I didn't know then that I was coming to the

19 Juin '06

Quenard, tabacs. — Corbeil

end of one journey and the beginning of a new adventure. Cast and crew would change on the *Julia Hoyt* and I would come home to a special place that would open its country kitchen doors to me and invite friends, family, and guests in.

The next hundred miles of meandering canal unfolded through a snowflake frame as I came to learn the quirks and turns of locks and aqueducts. It only snows once every ten years here. The strong southwestern sun soon melted the frost off the strawberries. The wild garlic and leeks began pushing their way up along the towpaths and the gardens were turned and planted as both the *Julia Hoyt* and I warmed to the people, farms, and villages of Gascony.

The first question most people ask me is "Whatever made you buy a canal barge?" I answer, "Romance." The romance of long voyages, overland safaris, and sea journeys, as well as the fabled French canals, inspired me to buy the *Julia Hoyt*. Traveling and cooking have always been interwoven as I learned to cook and eat manioc root in West Africa, conch chowder in the Antilles, and bitter winter salad greens in Tuscany. Like an escargot with its books, bags, and kitchen handy in its tidy steel shell, the *Julia Hoyt* inched across a continent. For every slow mile that I sailed discovering the countryside, new ideas and ways to cook unfolded, page by page, like the old strip charts of canals and rivers. Garlic gave way to shallots, orchards replaced vineyards, favored wines changed colors, then back again. Wild hare in onion sauce was replaced by farm rabbit cooked with prunes; after-dinner *digestives* changed from juniper berry to plum brandies. The local, very good wines, sold *en vrac* (in bulk and filled at gas station-type pumps) or as château-bottled vintages sampled and purchased at their source, began to fill the *cave* (wine cellar) of the *Julia Hoyt*. First through Champagne, where the Aisne meets the Marne River, then along the tree-shrouded Saône River, I discovered geography as well as wine labels. I bicycled the Beaujolais villages and memorized their names: Brouilly, Morgon, Fleurie, Moulin-À-Vent, Chénas, Juliénas, and Saint Amour. I sailed the *Julia Hoyt* through the treacherous arches of the medieval bridge at Mâcon and, with bright red Mâconnais wine, toasted St. Nicholas, patron saint of bargemen, safe in his bridge niche. Further south on the Rhône River, I walked the L'Hermitage and Châteauneuf de Pape vineyards before I found the Midi's Corbières and Minervois, and finally the vineyards of the great Southwest and Bordeaux.

When I had sailed the *Julia Hoyt* as far south and west as the canals allowed us to go into *la France profonde* (the hidden France), I found what awaited me in the rich culinary traditions of the agricultural valley of the Garonne River. In little more than one hundred miles of 60-foot-wide canal, I encountered a distinctive regional cooking based on farm and garden produce and adapted it to the limitations of my "bistro-galley." The local markets, farms, and friends I've discovered along the way have added their special Gascon character to the many meals served on the *Julia Hoyt*'s decks.

I began learning the cuisine of Southwest France in 1988, when I sailed into the wide Garonne River Valley. Since living here I've learned to cook and eat only by the seasons. Coming from California, a place where strawberries are available year-round and asparagus is cultivated for winter consumption, I had a lot to

learn. Here, the farm to market system in place for over 700 years has taught me not to buy artichokes in September or look for lamb in August. Instead, we eat our weight in sweet round melons in July, juicy strawberries in May, and wait for wild mushrooms when they arrive with the game in autumn. (Naturally, it is the game hunters scouting in the woods for wild hare or boar who find the hidden *cèpes*, Boletus edulis, and abundant *trompettes de la mort* or poor man's truffles.) Although preserving food is raised to a fine art in the confits of duck and pork, fruit jams, and pickled vegetables, life in the Garonne Valley still revolves around a farmer's calendar of successive harvests and seasonal bounty. It's very easy to make a seasonal menu in France; go to the morning farmers market and see what is available from the small producers.

Influenced by my quirky environment, my cooking changed. Unexpected towpath finds such as *aillets* (wild garlic shoots) or ripening blackberries contribute to the spontaneity of the menus in the bistro-galley. Friendly gossip in markets and villages and under shady trees adds twists to old favorite Gascon recipes. I, in turn, interpret this rustic *cuisine familiale* (home cooking) for our American guests as part of their immersion into the local culture of Gascony as they tour, cruise, and dine along the winding canal on weeklong charters.

The cooking of Southwest France is admittedly in vogue these days. From Paris and Nice to New York and San Francisco, restaurant menus reflect the rich history of a fertile farmland that produces not only the confits of duck and geese, but also the prized foie gras, *gésiers* (preserved gizzards), the air-dried, salt-cured hams, and the confection-like, slow-baked prunes steeped in armagnac and eau-de-vie. Here in the Southwest, along the Garonne River, there is little else but these time-honored traditions.

The "secret" of these succulent and satisfying menus is in maintaining a certain level of romance that I find in my long village. Not the hearts-and-flowers Valentine's Day type of romance, but the very simple and perfect pairing of wild thyme and bay leaf. Salty ham and sweet tomatoes marry with a healthy farm-raised fowl and simmer slowly with a glass of wine while family stories are told across a kitchen table.

In this traditional Gascon cuisine, the romance for me is in the honest and true ingredients of the cooking. It is not a fabrication of fancy ingredients piled high on one another like an overly constructed dessert in a fashionable top-dollar restaurant. Culinary romance is the sugary juices glazing a crusty tart made with apricots that just left the tree, and served with an afternoon cup of strong coffee at an oilcloth-covered kitchen table. I seek it in the ordinary and live out the fantasy as much as I can, and probably more than most. If, with these recipes that I teach in the Country Kitchens of Gascony tours, I can also impart some of that romance to your table, the experiences will be richer, the company more lively, and the tales more colorful as each plate is shared.

There have been other romances on this barge journey. I met my husband, Patrick Ratliffe, while moored at the Écluse de Sanglier (Lock of the Wild Boar) just east of Toulouse. On his first visit to France, Patrick was subjected, several times a day, to my bursting into poetic rapture about the noble history of barges, the romantic life of the *mariniers*, or bargemen, and the meandering rivers and arrow-straight waterways that crisscross the continent. I intro-duced him to the France that I loved; the France of big steel boats and 5,000 miles of inland waterways. Patrick, already an experienced skipper, caught my infatuation with my nearly eighty-year-old, sixty-five-ton Dutch barge and "the Commodore" signed on board. Now, together, we stop on bridges to watch a loaded *péniche* (canal barge) cruise below, hauling grain from our long village toward the sea. Patrick shares his love of history with us all and together we discover what ancient treasures lay hidden in the small farms and fortressed villages along the towpaths. We enjoy sharing with others the rituals that dictate the daily meals, the convivial pomp that elevates a midday meal into an event, the almost religious observation of the morning coffees, the evening aperitif hour, and the final salute of digestives after a meal.

I have learned much of what I know of these rituals and life in the long village from a family that lives in one of the smallest vil-

lages, called Lagruère. It was at the famous first Fête du Canal at Lagruère that we met the Pompèle family. Claude Pompèle was overseeing the construction of the temporary craft stalls and Vetou Pompèle was in charge of the French-style "box lunches"—a wooden fruit box overflowing with baguette, grilled *saucisse de Toulouse*, a whole sweet melon, *frites* (real french fries), an armagnac-perfumed apple tart, a wedge of cheese, and a bottle of red wine. Yannick Pompèle took our lines as we arrived and helped us moor to the too-big-to-hug plane trees. At first, the Pompèles were part of the smiling blur of faces that greeted us as we passed each village and farm. But it didn't take many trips through this modest community without bakery or shops until the tidy village house with its red-tiled *pigeonnier* (dovecote) and backyard full of crowing roosters, a donkey, and dozens of ducks started to stand apart. Claude opened the hand-chiselled door to the house that he built and the slow-simmering perfume of Vetou's kitchen invited us in.

One of the best home cooks in France, Vetou Pompèle has prepared for me, and for all aboard the *Julia Hoyt*, more meals, shared more recipes, and taught me the authentic cuisine of Gascony in her *façon Vetou* (Vetou's way). If they added a little wild celery leaf to a soup in the old days, Vetou walks outside her kitchen door to break off a lean branch or two and crushes it into the pot. If a recipe calls for a laying hen rather than for a fryer, then Vetou knows the farmer who has a "chee-kun" ready for Sunday's dinner. Like most good French cooks, she is full of *trucs* (tricks) that render straightly written down recipes almost impossible. Besides, it's much more fun to sit at the kitchen table with a glass of Claude's *vin de noix* (green walnut aperitif) and hear the stories that are interwoven with the ingredients.

This book is for fellow romantics interested in very regional and distinctive cuisine, prepared with seasons and geography in mind. It is not the definitive book on the cooking of Gascony. It is not the ultimate travel guide to Southwest France. Rather, this is a personal travel tale of the people and cuisine of my long village. This cookbook is a journey aboard the *Julia Hoyt* with me and Patrick and all the friends and guests that share our love of lively tables and good food. Above all, this is a European Culinary Adventure. Welcome aboard!

AT HOME ON THE *JULIA HOYT*:

A River, a Valley, a Canal, and a Barge

A RIVER

FROM THE WORLD-famous Bordeaux vineyards of Sauternes, Graves, and Entre-Deux-Mers to the market-basket farms and gardens that supply France and much of Europe with tomatoes, strawberries, lettuces, peppers, potatoes, and fruit, the Garonne River dictates life. One of the four important river basins in France (La Seine, La Loire, and Le Rhône are the others), La Garonne is sometimes called the last wild river in Europe. On gray November days when she is in flood and an angry muddy red tide of whole trees crashes into bridge pilings, she earns her title.

I call the Garonne the "mother river" not just because she is a feminine waterway (*La* Garonne), but because as she flows northwest to her rendezvous with the sea, she gathers in the Ariege, the Save, the Gimone, the Tarn, the Arrats, the Gers, the Baïse, the Lot, the Drot, the Ciron, and a hundred other rivulets. La Garonne then joins with La Dordogne, well past the grand city of Bordeaux, to become La Gironde, the wide western estuary where, influenced by incoming tides, she washes backwards and forwards across a salty silt-brown bottom. This "mothering" made La Garonne the main waterway for transporting all the goods grown and gathered along these rivers—Bordeaux wines, armagnac, timber, cork, grain. It also subjected her to major flooding several times a century. In geological time, this accounts for the long, looping horseshoe bends and fertile fields from Toulouse to Bordeaux as

La Garonne regularly overflowed its banks, changed course, and deposited rich layers of soil again and again.

On a summer day where I now see fields of ripening tomatoes, tasseling corn, and the all-important *potager* (the home vegetable garden), I remember pear trees standing in a lake like an orchard island and rowboats shuttling farmers and their families across lost fields. In one's short lifetime, this occasional flooding seems a small, if dramatic, price to pay for the bounty that this rich land produces.

When the river sirens wailed from the village church late one rainy night, I saw with new eyes the farmhouses built up on earthen berms, testimony to the practical and tenacious cultivators of this fertile land. Safe and secure on the quiet canal I learned to count the long and short signals that shouted the rising meter marks. Seven meters, eight meters, then nine and a half. La Garonne crested at ten meters, one meter shy of spilling into the canal.

A Valley

Out of these occasional bouts with the rampaging river come the dark chocolate fields that produce the crisp vegetables, sweet fruit, poultry, and other products that travel directly from farm to market in the Garonne Valley. Although there is commercialization on a wide scale now, most of the produce and meats available in the small village markets have not seen cold storage and hormone injections and I don't have to look very hard to find tiny, crisp *cornichons* for pickling or tree-ripened peaches to melt into *confitures* (preserves).

In neighboring farms and village homes along the canal, I have been taught the little trucs: an offhand toss of herbed sea salt, an infusion of mint, a blend of orange flower water and armagnac to perfume cakes, crêpes, and tarts. But more than all of these personal touches, techniques, and tricks, I have learned the real secret of French country cooking: the country itself. The French use the word *terroir*, earth, to answer the questions: why do these grapes taste different here and there, why is this chicken so tasty here, these white peaches more perfumed here, those beans soft and sweet, that melon different, that garlic better? The answer is always the land itself. Here, in the wide valley with its fertile, flood-plain farms, the Garonne River contributes again and again to this fruitful earth.

A CANAL

The Canal Latéral à la Garonne, and all the villages on its banks, runs along-side La Garonne from the brick red city of Toulouse, lively with a distinct southern flair, toward the inland ocean port of Bordeaux, elegant in carved limestone and classic architecture. The 100-plus miles of canal gently spill downstream by a series of ever-descending locks until the harnessed waters tumble into the tidal Garonne River at Castets-en-Dorthe, thirty miles upstream from Bordeaux. In and out of villages, bisecting farms and crossing fields, the mirrored canal reflects a hundred different greens as it straightens out the horseshoe bends of La Garonne that loop dizzily across its own broad valley.

On a week's journey, we stop at Agen for its market, Serignac-sur-Garonne for its bakery, Buzet-sur-Baïse to buy wine. The next day we post a letter in Damazan, have a glass of cold rosé in a canal-side cafe, then moor in tiny Lagruère to have dinner with friends on the weekend. This is the wet road the *Julia Hoyt* takes again and again as the history and stories of the canal come to life at 8 kilometers an hour.

First-time guests are always surprised at the intricacies and history of the hand-built canals, the great stone locks holding thousands of gallons of water, and the manually operated doors and gateways that allow us to ascend or descend the 600 feet of elevation between the Atlantic Ocean and the Mediterranean Sea. We marvel at the early engineering, at the reservoirs, gates, paddles, and channels that were the product of one man's vision over 300 years ago.

Pierre-Paul Riquet started his Canal du Midi in 1666. His imagination and determination exceeded technological limits as he linked the then navigable Garonne River at Toulouse with the Mediterranean port of Sète. The hand-dug

240-kilometer canal was built in an astonishingly quick fifteen years. But the Garonne River still caused navigational problems. Not until 1865, some 199 years after the inauguration of the Canal du Midi, would the Canal Latéral à la Garonne complete the project long dreamed of by Roman emperors and French kings, a cross-continental link that would eliminate a dangerous sea voyage of 1,800 miles around the Iberian peninsula. By this time, however, a new age had begun and the railroad was waiting on the towpath to compete with barge traffic. The Canal du Midi, never modernized to the Freycinet standard of the twentieth century, failed to admit the standard thirty-nine-meter péniches. Commercial traffic on the Latéral à la Garonne was choked off and has eventually dwindled to a few persevering *bateliers*.

Grand-mère Yvette, a canal-side neighbor at Ste. Colombe, told me that when

she was a girl, there was a loaded péniche passing every half hour, all day and every day. When I arrived here in 1988, only two dozen commercial barges hauled grain, fuel, and wine. Now there are four somber barges—the *Babette, Storm, Drakkar,* and *Barran*—that keep the pilot alert on corners and contribute to the automatic dredging of the channel as they pass fully loaded at 350 tons, their large propellers churning the bottom free and keeping the canal from silting up.

A BARGE

A leaf falls onto this placid canal and the stillness of the mirrored surface breaks into patterns of circles and rings. The boat itself is like a leaf, as she disturbs the flat surface with her slow and deliberate movement. Barely leaving a wake, the grasses and towpath trees are troubled for only seconds as the ponderous *Julia Hoyt* cruises by. Greens

of every hue echo
across the banks, and
the overhead shadows
of leaves flipping in the
southwest wind dapple
this long, quiet strand
of shallow water.

The boats built to
sail the canals and
inland waters are stur-
dy vessels of wood and
steel, heavy and slow-
moving. Whether
hauling goods or converted to pleasure craft, like the *Julia Hoyt*, they inspire an
inland-nautical madness reflected in their polished brass, spotless steel decks,
and tidy living quarters. I have now seen hundreds of barges, river boats, and
canal cruisers, and I am hopelessly contented with our *Julia Hoyt*. When Patrick
and I compare the finer points of the deck space on that péniche or the paint job
on that *luxemotor*, I stand smug in my passion for this old boat. "Look, they've let
that lovely old Belgian barge start to rust!" I head for the anti-rust primer.
"What a nice garden the *Mosan* has." I quietly add some houseplant fertilizer to
my pots of lavender and pansies.

Never having been a dedicated housekeeper, I amaze myself with the joy I
take at polishing the knotty pine planking, waxing the handpainted antique
buffets, ironing the mountains of bed and table linens. I glow enthusiastically at
the prospect of unplugging a blocked water hose. I volunteer to dive in the chill
water to check the rudder. I take the water pump apart with a satisfaction akin
to mothering an orphaned wild animal, then I scrub the grease out from under
my nails. "*Voilà*. I fixed that!" I call it the big boat malady.

Most Americans call the *Julia Hoyt* a barge. The French say *péniche* and the Dutch
call her by her proper name, a *tjalk*. I call her "the boat." She was built in Friesland
in the Netherlands in the middle of World War I. As a twenty-five-meter sailing
tjalk, she moved cargoes of grain, lumber, thatching, and coal through the narrow
canals and vast inland seas under her tanbark sails. Modern cargo barges, motor-

propelled or push-towed, still move millions of tons of goods over thousands of kilometers of waterways from Eastern Europe to the giant inland ports of Antwerpen and Rotterdam. The *Julia Hoyt* originally had a great gaff-rigged main sail, a small mizzen mast, and was balanced on both sides by a pair of thick, wooden leeboards. These teardrop-shaped leeboards acted as her keel when under sail. Now, without them, she is as slippery in a little breeze as an eighty-five-foot bar of wet soap. One puff of wind and over to the wrong side of the canal she goes. I know little about her early history other than she was built in 1916 and wasn't "modernized" until 1938, when a diesel engine was put in. Thirty years later she was taken out of commercial trade and converted to a pleasure boat for a Dutch family. I bought her in 1986 with a friend, moved on board the following spring, and began the second conversion, one that would turn her into a luxury-class vessel.

I remember the first time that I returned to San Francisco after buying the *Julia Hoyt* and passed her photographs around the room like a new mother. A collective sigh filled the air and the silence was broken by a friend. "Oh, thank God, Kate. We thought you had bought a World War II landing barge!" Everyone agreed she was beautiful. So the *Julia Hoyt* entered my family like an adopted child and presents of old lace and linens, silver trays, and a lovely German clock christened her maiden voyages. My own biological clock was drowned out by the steady rhythm of the 120 horsepower engine as I entered a new world of heavy machine-driven cruising. Still as a house in even the most violent weather, the *Julia Hoyt* is my safe haven and a magic talisman to another world.

Stable in the water, fourteen feet wide, and displacing sixty-five tons, this floating *auberge* (inn) barely rocks in the water. She has two bedrooms for guests and two for the crew. The two guest rooms are comfortable, with big beds and rows of books, portholes, hatches, and other nautical touches to remind landlubbers that this is a boat and not just a cozy hotel. She has two marine bathrooms that work by pumps, and plenty of storage in all the nooks and crannies underneath varnished pine floorboards and painted steel decks. The wheelhouse shelters the pilot from sun or storm and is a favored gathering spot for lunch. The cushioned banquette

BISTRO-GALLEY TOOLS

   2 1-quart saucepans
   2 2-quart saucepans
   1 3-quart saucepan
   1 12-inch sauteuse, 4 inches deep with a tight-fitting lid (large enough for a whole chicken)
   1 12-quart stock pot
   1 large (10-15-quart) *toupin*, a fat-bellied pot used to cook beans, potatoes, etc.
   1 6-inch sauté pan
   assorted terra-cotta glazed casseroles (I look for these in secondhand shops)
   individual-sized oven-proof ramekins
   single-serving tart pans
   medium and large tart pans (tart pans are shallow (3/4-inch), fluted-edged baking pans made of steel, aluminum, glass, or ceramic)
   food processor and blender
   hand mixer for puréeing soups
   whisks
   wooden spoons
   12-inch tongs
   French rolling pin (a solid baton of wood)
   sharp Japanese carbon steel knives
   screwdriver (for fixing pot handles and other handy work)
   Swiss army knife
   scissors
   kitchen twine

I also have four sets of dishes, three sets of cutlery, and assorted silver serving dishes and platters. Anything lovely and old that can used to serve with is stored in the hand-painted buffet.

hides my art supplies, souvenirs of Africa, and all the unfinished projects that I thought I would do in my spare time. ("My spare time" is the most-favored joke on the boat!) Our captain's cabin in the aft is roomy and *never* organized, with the bath wedged in between the engine room and the toilet. The crew sleeps forward in the fo'c'sle, the foxhole, underneath a ceiling of glow-in-the-dark stars.

I call my kitchen on the *Julia Hoyt* the bistro-galley. Open for all to see, it is a tight-fitting puzzle of a kitchen separated from the salon by an elbow-high bar that serves as a comfortable barrier from the sometimes chaotic activities behind the scenes. The traditionally slow Gascon farm cooking is often interrupted by the hectic schedule of the chef who has to change hats to become pilot when a lock looms into view or has to suddenly leave the kitchen when all hands are needed for the afternoon's mooring even though a cake is in the oven.

Every dinner has a tale in this storytelling kitchen. I tell the pieces of history as I cook, my dinner guests listening as they perch at the galley bar. Bits of onion are sliced into a pot shiny with duck fat as we talk of crusaders and kings. Eggs are beaten for fluid *crèmes* over the farmwife gossip of the next village. The bistro-galley is my personal theater—a fresh white apron and hat is the costume, well-used spoons and pots are the props. I write the menus on the window behind the stove like little plays and give them names to reflect the stories they tell of the area. "The Great Garonne" is a dinner of freshly caught *alose* (shad). "A Gascon Farm" is the slowly-stewed barnyard guinea hen with fresh garden vegetables.

The bistro-galley will never be finished, as each year brings another good idea on using the limited space. The *brocante* (junk store) finds like the little carved kitchen buffet had to be accommodated, as did the highly eccentric but practical marine kerosene refrigerator. The shallow, single sink basin handles all the dishes and wine glasses from three meals a day for seven people and the bilge pantry stores fresh produce underneath the floorboards among the cool stainless steel water tanks. I prepare these recipes on a regular basis here, elbow to elbow with the other crew. If I can cook four-course dinners with a midget-sized gas range, a single too-small sink, and no counter space on a moving boat, then believe me, you can cook them, too. As a friend once told me, "It's not about equipment, Kate."

Bright with light from the eight large picture windows, the salon and the bistro-galley have an unrivaled view of the shy creatures that inhabit the canal— great herons, kingfishers, and chanting frogs. The *poule d'eau* (moor hen) calls from hiding and a little walnut of downy black scoots to her side, cheeping.

The not-so-wildlife on this canal is as animated as characters from a children's book. I wait for the first spotting of a cranky crayfish or the salute of a solemn heron on its long canal flight. The raucous frogs compete like chattering monkeys or honking geese as we laugh and make merry on a summer evening. South American nutria settle into their adopted French burrows on the canal banks; their nocturnal antics on the rudder of the *Julia Hoyt* herald spring. The little forest at Camont, our canal-side farm, is an aviary of song from March until mid-July; August hushes the thick layer of tree-rustling birds. If I sit long enough and still enough to see the starlight reflected in the canal's unruffled water, the pair of dame blanche barn owls from the pigeonnier may silently glide up the towpath in search of midnight snacks. The *Julia Hoyt* may be one of the largest things on the canal, but the smaller population is often more active. The view from my galley window onto the towpath reveals the antics of a pesky mole burrowing up under the gangplank and his helter-skelter blind dash as he seeks the dark again.

The long village isn't just the towns, people, and creatures that live on the banks of the canal. It is the canal itself and the people and boats that travel on it. Some days it is quiet and we cruise without passing another soul. Other days it is a parade of new and old friends saluting as they pass or stopping to share a visit. Generations of bargees moving huge cargoes nod and wave. A bottle of favorite wine is exchanged, wrapped to a bargepole with duct tape. Australians Arthur and Betty on the *Pommes*, their English narrowboat, stop for a cup of coffee and to catch up in passing on their way to Narbonne for the winter. A Nordic couple on the sailing yacht *Rissa* rafts up to the *Julia Hoyt* as a violent thunderstorm passes over. We speak briefly of philosophy and food until the clouds lift and our friends continue toward Greece. I wave them off and return to caramelizing potatoes for an early supper. Ocean-going kayaks, camping canoes, outboard-powered "mosquito" boats, yachts, catamarans, even an oar-rowed Russian galley from the Black Sea, her elegantly painted eyes on each side of the prow, have sailed through my long village on the way to the sea. The legacy of hundreds of years of work and travel on the Garonne River and her canal has been shared with all of us travelers by the lockkeepers and bargemen preserving their slowly disappearing way of life. These barges and boats, once as distinctively regional as the cuisine, are the raison d'être for the long village.

CASTETS·EN·DORTHE

A Barge Town

SOUVENIR IS THE French word for "memory" and "to remember." *Je souviens...* I remember well the long and slow voyage that led me and this antique canal boat from the very north of Holland to the furthest southwest point of the French canals—the barge town, Castets-en-Dorthe. Now we begin most of our trips here.

If you start counting from Lock #1, Écluse de Lalande, leaving the Canal du Midi at Toulouse, then Lock #53, Écluse de Castets, at Castets-en-Dorthe, is technically the end of the Canal Latéral à la Garonne. Here the miles of slow canals are left behind and the river Garonne is navigable to the sea. Like a terraced staircase down to the river, locks # 53, #52, and #51 gently lower loaded barges and ocean-going sailboats onto the wide tidal Garonne as it makes its way northwest to the riverport city Bordeaux, and then to the Atlantic. But the *Julia Hoyt* stops here between the last locks of the canal, Écluse de Gares and Écluse de Mazerac. It was here in a then-crowded port of barges that I learned about many important beginnings. I learned about barge life as it was in the beginning on this now quiet waterway. I learned about the beginning of this wide Garonne River Valley and why it is the bountiful and fertile garden of southwestern France.

Castets-en-Dorthe sits above the nineteenth-century locks and the timeless river. Solemn gray Château DuHamel, built in the mid-1300s, perches on the edge

8. - CASTETS-en-DORTHE (Gironde). - Le Can...

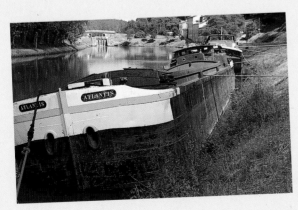

ECLUSE 47
DES GRAVIERES
BERNES | AURIOLE
2478ᵐ | 7489ᵐ

of town over the river as if still hosting those medieval barons waiting to swoop down and extract tolls from passing vessels for Pope Clement V at Avignon. Still in private hands, this many-towered château remains silent and mysterious as the townsfolk carry out the business of everyday village life beneath its shadow. As in so many other river ports, the history of Castets is written along the banks of the Garonne across centuries of commerce: fish, cargo, transport. Nowadays, Castets-en-Dorthe is nearly asleep, like so many other canal ports and villages. The bakery opens late on weekends, the butcher closes early in hunting season, and the giant grain barges doze in the forgotten port.

But once there was another prosperous town at Castets, equally important and full of history, a barge town. It wasn't long ago that some 300 commercial  cargo barges hauled their goods from the Canal du Midi inland through Toulouse to the seaport at Bordeaux. Now we see just four slow-moving barges hauling grain and fuel between the country and the city. Where the canal comes to its close there is a graceful sweeping port that at one time housed most of the fleet of barges that hauled on the canal and the Garonne. Moored nose to tail and seven or eight abreast, flags flying and laundry fluttering, this "barge town," like others throughout France, moved and breathed with daily maritime and domestic activities. Whole families lived on their working boats and, in community with others, lived and breathed the cargo trade. Children, when old enough, boarded at the local school. Laundry hung from the aft lines or along trees beside the canal. Meals were shared *en famille* in the tiny rear cabins that served as kitchen, salon, bedroom, and toilet. In summer, the towpath became the meeting place for aperitifs and gossip, work news, and flirting. Marriages of barge daughters to barge sons were feted with flags and flower-bedecked boats as the close community reinforced its future and tightened the knots. From father to son and mother to daughter, bargees are born, not apprenticed.

It's so much quieter now. When I first came to the end of what would become my long village, there were a dozen or more giant thirty-nine-meter barges working from Castets. Six years later, the few remaining boats, tethered to the towpath with telephone and electrical lines, rest like retired circus ele-

phants. Those last survivors of a three-hun-
dred-year-old tradition echo the names of
the past: *Atlantis, Drakkar, Karim, Motus,*
Fion, Barran, Calypso, Storm, Zambezi, Esperance,
Bacchus, Babette. I love those names. They are
as heroic as befits a 320-ton, 120-foot-long
self-propelled river craft.

Flat-bottomed and boxy, modern French
barges are designed to hold every possible
last grain of corn that is destined for the
giant silos past Bordeaux. Yet, look again at
the large steel working vessels. Behind the
neatly furled coils of docking lines, fluttering flags, and brightly polished brass bells
lies a less nautical demeanor: delicate lace
curtains trim the captain's cabin windows, a
canary sings in its brass cage in the wheelhouse, and a pot of scarlet geraniums
perches on the aft deck. The last *bateliers*
(bargemen) of Castets are an extended family protective and proud of their vessels.

Victor and Yvonne
of the Babette

One evening when we had guests
aboard at Castets, I found myself with an
overabundance of finger foods prepared for the aperitif hour.
My guests were sated and ready for the next course, and, loath
to toss the remaining goodies overboard or store them in the
already overflowing refrigerator, I spotted the group of familiar
bargees that had gathered for a friendly *pastis* or a *rivesaltes* at
the sturdy wooden table beside their barges.

"*Bonsoir, messieurs-dames.* Would you like to try some American *apéros*?"

The silence was shocking. Other than "*bonjour*" and a courtesy nod of recogni-
tion when passing on the canal, this tight-knit group had never ventured a conversation with the captain and cook of the *Julia Hoyt* before. Pierre of *Motus*, Jean-
Marc of *Calypso*, and several Jean-Louis eyed the loaded platter in hand before

Victor, captain of the *Babette*, with a gourmand's glint in his eye proclaimed a boisterous, *"Beh, oui!"* Yvonne, his enthusiastic first mate and wife, piped up, *"Pourquoi pas?"* (why not?), and the rest of the normally taciturn clan came to life around the savory morsels of garlicky toasts, flaky pastry shells filled with tomatoes, salty anchovies and capers topped with crème fraîche, and dabs of pâté on crusty squares of bread. In return for this unexpected offering, the entire crew of the *Julia Hoyt* was invited to a bargee breakfast the next morning (yes, the French do eat breakfast!) and thus began the first of many culinary exchanges between barge and boat. Later, we sailed the rushing Garonne River with Victor and Yvonne on the *Babette* when she was loaded with 320 tons of corn, and toasted the honor of all bargemen (and bargewomen!) everywhere. Amongst this last generation of Gascon bargees, I enjoy a reputation as a good cook, an honor bestowed upon me thanks to a simple platter of aperitifs.

APERITIFS

In France, and especially on the *Julia Hoyt*, the aperitif hour is a simple ritual of food and drink and switching of gears from work or play to the more serious matters of dining and conversation. Originating from a medical term, *"apéritif"* now signifies the opening ceremony that stimulates the desire for more. *"Apéros"* is slang for particular drinks and foods that signal the mind and the digestive system that a meal is about to begin. Aperitifs are the real first course of a typical French meal.

Aperitif drinks are aromatic and often sweet, like the anise-based pastis Pernod. They can be herbal, like the gentian root-based Suze, or wines fortified with alcohol, *vins cuits* (cooked wines) like St. Raphaël and Rivesaltes. In America, we are familiar with Dubonnet, Vermouth, and Lillet, made popular at the turn of the century. But in France, the list of familiar and popular aperitifs is as varied as any good wine list. Although American cocktails are popular in city bars, obscure regional specialties like Ratafia, Byrrh, and Banyuls pop up in village cafes, homes, and farms. In the countryside I have tasted drinks made from twigs, leaves, and fruit. Whatever is local, bitter, and in abundance can be made into a favored *"apéritif maison."*

Aperitifs come in many flavors and reflect the French penchant for herbs and spices. Victor (of the *Babette*) favors his pastis flavored with mint, locally called *un perroquet* (a parrot). I once used a delicate rosemary syrup I found in a village market to make a flute of champagne into a *kir jardin*. But my all-time favorite aperitif to drink is the homemade *vin de noix* made from green walnuts, eau-de-vie (brandy), and good rosé wine that our friend Claude Pompèle offers us when we arrive on his doorstep in the little village of Lagruère. Claude's aperitif is legendary among our American guests, not so much for the kick it packs but for the introduction to life beyond bottles with labels. In the long village, anything homemade has extra magic and to start a French meal with the most French of all rituals, the homemade aperitif, is especially valued.

If I teach just one thing to all the friends who have supped with us on the *Julia Hoyt*, it's that aperitifs come first as we stop to moor along the banks at the end of an eventful day. Savoring the mood changes from day to dusk, from industry to leisure, we learn to anticipate the rest of the meal to come.

The finger foods that accompany aperitifs stimulate the appetite, too, and are a salty contrast to the sweet drinks. Any bar will serve you some nicely roasted, salted peanuts in a small saucer or a little pot of pungent green olives to taste as you sip a Ricard or Berger Blanc (two brands of pastis), a Frontignan or Rivesaltes (fortified wines from near the Mediterranean), or perhaps a newly-in-vogue whisky (scotch to us). But walk inside a French home or gather on the deck of a boat or along the canal towpath, and the variations of food and drink are many and far more interesting.

Gathered around the bar on the *Julia Hoyt*, aperitif foods can be as lean as a few buttery crackers on which to nibble or as substantial as a filled pastry shell *tourte*, small sausages skewered with prunes and then grilled, or a jar of homemade pâté and cornichons served with toast. I adjust my offerings to the schedule at hand, the appetites of the crew, and the time needed to prepare dinner. Food and drink are never so abundant that they satisfy the appetite; rather they are the highly ritualized introduction to the meal. Aperitifs must always be finished before dinner begins.

APERITIF ETIQUETTE

One summer's day, in the port of Castets-en-Dorthe, I learned the ultimate aperitif food lesson, from Jerome, then twelve, born and raised on the barge *Motus*. Oars splashed expertly, showering us with cooling spray. The canal was as warm as a bath. We spoke in schoolyard French,

less interested in verb forms than in jokes. After a lazy row around the port in his little green boat, Jerome asked if he could help me with dinner. Eager to remain in his unaffected and charming company, I recruited him as sous-chef for the evening. We tied the plastic dinghy alongside the *Julia Hoyt* and scrambled up a tire fender to stand dripping on the deck. In the bistro-galley, I began to unwrap, set out, and open jars to assemble a mosaic of savory bits on a large silver tray. Jerome eyed with interest the *tapenade* spread made of black olives and anchovies, the giant salted capers that I'd brought back from Italy, the little jar of local caviar made from sturgeon caught at the mouth of the great Garonne River. But when I started slicing a large, crumbly block of Cantal cheese from the mountainous region northeast of Toulouse, this young boy, who knows as much about haute cuisine as I know about space technology, looked me in the eye and said, "*Fromage...maintenant?*" (Cheese...NOW?) Stunned, I swiftly rewrapped the pale block of cheddar-like cheese as if I had lost my head for a minute. Whatever was I thinking? I must have had a momentary culture lapse! "Of course not," I sighed. "Cheese? At this hour?" Whew. Young Jerome saved me from the embarrassing fate of presenting the much-coveted after-dinner course before the meal had even begun. In France, even a twelve-year-old knows that first things come first, especially aperitifs!

VIN DE NOIX
Green Walnut Aperitif
Makes 2 liters

It isn't a visit to chez Pompèle unless we share an aperitif of our friend Claude Pompèle's homemade walnut-flavored fortified wine. This *apéritif maison* (house drink) is perfected every year as family and friends critique, judge, compliment, and, most of all, enjoy the bitter-fragrant sweet wine.

In midsummer, St. Jean's Eve is celebrated in the country with bonfires lit in steel boats and set afloat along the Garonne. This very old custom is feted in villages with special dinners and a *bal musette* (town dance). This is the day

Claude picks the walnuts from the tree. Green walnuts are the husk, shell, and kernel of the walnut in its immature phase. When you cut a fruit in half, you can see the outline of the nut just starting to form in the juicy white flesh. Smash the walnuts outside wearing your old work clothes since the tannins in the nut will stain everything dark brown. Vetou says that French women used to "tan" their legs with walnut juice during the war when silk stockings were in short supply.

21 green walnuts picked on a mid-summer day (traditionally June 24, St. Jean's Day)
1 pint (16 fl oz / 500 ml) eau-de-vie (plain fruit brandy) or vodka
1 1/2 cups (12 oz / 300 g) sugar
3 bottles (2 liters) good red or rosé wine
1/4 teaspoon ground cinnamon or 1 cinnamon stick
several gratings whole nutmeg
3 whole cloves
zest of 1 lemon

1. Cut and smash the whole walnuts with a rolling pin on an old piece of wood. Gloves are needed as the green nuts will stain everything they touch. Smash the milky fruit well. Place in an earthenware crock or plastic bucket with a lid. This is messy but fun business!

2. Add the rest of the ingredients to the crock and stir well until the sugar is dissolved.

3. Let rest about a month in a cool, dark place, then strain through several layers of cheesecloth (I used a paper coffee filter once with good results). Pour into bottles, and cork. Store the bottles vertically so the alcohol won't eat the cork.

4. Serve chilled in a little sherry glass. *Salut, à nous!*

VIN CUIT
Cooked Spiced Wine
Serves 4

If vin de noix is a summer-type aperitif served cold and singing of summer days, then vin cuit is its wintertime equivalent—warm, spicy, and cozy. Just as we owe Claude Pompèle thanks for his walnut aperitif on our visits, it's Vetou Pompèle who is the instigator in these cool autumn days as she wraps a violet-flowered scarf around her neck and shivers for effect. "Let's cook some wine. It's good for warding off *la grippe*." Vin cuit is also delicious in the summer if you chill it with ice and add a little fruit for a French-style sangria. This is a refreshingly soft and spicy wine.

1 bottle (750 ml) full-bodied red wine (in France, I would use a bottle of home-made farm wine or a good *vin de table*)
1/4 cup (2 oz/60 g) granulated sugar
zest from 1 lemon and 1 orange
1 cinnamon stick
1 piece vanilla bean
1 or 2 whole cloves
1/2 cup (4 fl oz/125 ml) armagnac, cognac, brandy, or eau-de-vie

1. Place the wine in a noncorrosive saucepan. Bring it to a simmer. The surface will be covered with small bubbles. Flame the wine using a long match and let it "cook" until the flames go out.

2. Add the sugar, zest, spices, and armagnac, and continue to cook at a lively simmer for a minute or two.

3. Remove from heat and cover. Let the spices infuse the wine for three to five minutes, then strain and serve very hot. If you prefer it cool, pour into a carafe and refrigerate, or chill in an ice bucket. Serve cold, using a slice of fruit as a garnish.

MES OLIVES PRÉFÉRÉES
My Special Olives

On top of the kerosene refrigerator in the bistro-galley are jars and bottles of all sizes of oils and vinegars, condiments, and olives. The fastest aperitif food in town comes from the tall jar toward the back with the clamped-down glass lid: my olives. I put a cupful of these shiny, plump black berries in a hand-blown glass bowl and set it next to the aperitif tray. Whoosh, they start to disappear, the pits launched into the canal. Before long, someone says, "These are so good. What kind of olives are they?" "My olives," I say as I casually spoon a few more to the bowl. "I just add a few herbs to them." This is how I really make them!

2 cups (16 oz/500 g) plain black olives, Greek or Italian style
2 shallots, whole or sliced
4-5 cloves garlic, barely crushed
fresh or dried herbs: thyme, rosemary, fennel seeds, chives, sage
juice of 1/2 fresh lemon
Worcestershire sauce
Tabasco sauce or hot pepper flakes
1 cup (8 fl oz/250 ml) olive oil

1. Place the olives in a jar with a tight-fitting lid.
2. Add to the jar shallots, garlic cloves, a handful of fresh or dried herbs chopped or left whole, lemon juice, a few shakes of Worcestershire sauce, and a few drops of Tabasco or shakes of hot pepper flakes.
3. Pour olive oil to cover the olives and herbs and seal the lid. Shake a couple of times to mix all ingredients well. Leave these olives to plump in the oil and absorb the perfume of the herbs. As you use them replenish the stock with more olives in the same oil mixture until it at last seems too tired to do the job. The herb-scented oil is then perfect for brushing on grilled foods as they finish or in other cooking.

TAPENADE VERTE
Green Olive Spread
Serves 6

Although I usually have a jar of black olive tapenade readymade in the pantry, I improvised this recipe one day based on what I *did* have in the cupboard and presented a fast, fresh hors d'oeuvre for aperitif hour. I left the anchovies out of the recipe because the salad olives were salty enough. Let your taste buds dictate! Black olives can be used (Greek or Italian rather than the watery-tasting canned American olives). Remember to remove the pits. Any brine or oil-cured olive will work, adjusting seasoning as needed. Anchovies will intensify the flavor.

1 12 oz (350 g) jar pitted green salad olives, drained
1 shallot, peeled, halved, and chopped finely
1 squeeze fresh lemon juice (about 1 tsp)
freshly ground pepper, to taste
1/2 cup (4 fl oz/125 ml) olive oil
4 to 6 anchovy filets, optional
1 handful chopped chives

  1. In a food processor or small mixer, combine olives, shallot, lemon juice, pepper, and half of the olive oil. Add anchovies if desired.

  2. Pulse-blend until the mixture is a coarse paste consistency. Use more oil if necessary. I like to vary the coarseness according to what I am going to serve. A coarser consistency is good for vegetable crudités (a basket of green onions, fennel slices, cherry tomatoes). A smoother tapenade is good spread on thin slices of baguette, toasted, or thicker chunks of sourdough bread. For a smoother tapenade, use all of the olive oil and blend until creamy and smooth. Top with a sprinkling of chives and serve.

O L I V E

Floc: an armagnac-based aperitif similar to the Cognac region's Pineau des Charentes and found only in Gascony.

Pousse Rapière: an orange-scented armagnac liqueur combined with sparkling wine.

Kir Gascon: a local version of the classic Burgundian aperitif using crème de Mure (blackberry liqueur) and red wine.

Pastis: Brands include Pernod, Ricard, Berger Blanc, and 51 as well as generic versions simply labeled Pastis.

Dubonnet, Lillet, Vermouth: turn-of-the-century flavored and fortified wines, often containing quinine.

Suze: a gentian root-based bitters

Rivesaltes, St. Raphaël, Muscat de Frontignan, Byrrh: Fortified wines made near the Mediterranean with grapes grown in poor, sandy soil.

Vin de noix, vin de pêche, vin d'orange, vin de verveine: homemade wine-based drinks flavored with the leaves and/or fruit of walnuts, peaches, oranges, and lemon verbena, then sweetened and fortified with clear brandy.

LES RÔTIES SALÉES
Roasted Bread with Herbed Sea Salt
Serves 6 — 8

A French version of Italian *crostini*, these simple *rôties* are perfect when perfect ingredients are used. Use only hearty bread, sliced thickly with a rough knife, and a special fat like clean, white, mildly nutty duck fat rendered for *confits* or the buttery yellow fat of foie gras, rendered when it is canned in tins or jars. I never wash a jar that foie gras or pâté has come from without saving the flavorful fat left behind for cooking. Fruity olive oil or even a high-quality nut oil like walnut or hazelnut could be drizzled on the warm toast. The best unsalted butter could be used, of course. The herbed sea salt is one I make in August after a visit to the Île de Ré on France's Atlantic coast. The sea salt is hand-harvested and not bleached or processed in any way. I gather herbs from my garden and kitchen cupboards and combine with the coarse *fleurs de sel* (salt flowers) in old jam jars.

I use this herbed salt in lots of my dishes as this is the quickest way to recall the salt spray taste on the Île de Ré after we return to inland waters.

SALTED TOASTS

1 loaf French bread, a baguette, or a small round loaf
4 tablespoons duck fat, sweet butter, or olive oil
1 tablespoon herbed sea salt (see page 33)

1. Preheat the oven to 425 degrees F (220 C) or use the broiler in the oven, a stove burner, the barbecue, or the fireplace (the best of all!).

2. Texture is the key word here. Rough-cut the bread in 3/4-inch (2 cm) slices, and spread with a scant teaspoon of fat. Sprinkle with the herbed salt. Bake in the oven for ten minutes or until lightly browned, or toast under broiler, over a burner, or on grill.

3. Serve warm as everyone stands around the kitchen. A more elegant presentation would be to toast little chunks of bread torn in 1-inch (3 cm) square cubes. Using a pastry brush, spread one side with barely melted butter and dip in salt and herb mixture. Toss in a bowl and garnish with several peppery red radishes.

Caviar d'Aubergines
Eggplant Pâté
Serves 6—8

This tasty appetizer is often referred to as vegetarian pâté, but I prefer the more poetic French name given to eggplant when prepared as a pâté or spread: caviar. The eggplants are slowly cooked in their skins, either baked in the oven or grilled over an open flame, as when roasting red peppers. The pâté can be spread on toast or served as a dip with fresh vegetables.

1 large or 2 to 3 small eggplants (*aubergines*)
1/2 cup (4 oz/120 g) pitted black olives, chopped
3 to 4 cloves garlic, minced
juice of 1/2 fresh lemon
2 tablespoons olive oil
salt and freshly ground pepper to taste (2 to 3 anchovy filets can be substituted for the salt)

1. Preheat oven to 400 degrees F (200 C).
2. Place whole eggplants (aubergines) on a baking sheet and bake in the pre-heated oven for thirty to forty-five minutes. Alternately, you can roast the egg-plants by placing them over the open flame of the stovetop or grill, or under a broiler, and turning them often until done. The skins will be black and papery and the inside flesh soft.
3. Remove the eggplants from the heat and place inside a paper or plastic bag. Let cool.
4. Once cool, remove the eggplants and peel the black-ened skin off, using a knife if needed. Mash the eggplant flesh in a bowl with the rest of the ingredients. It can be coarsely

E G G P L A N T S

mashed with a fork if used to top slices of toast. Use a food processor to make a smoother paste to use as a dip. Serve from a bowl garnished with a drizzle of olive oil and cracked pepper, or spread on slices of grilled bread.

BARQUES DE CATALAN
Red Pepper and Anchovy Boats
Serves 6 — 8

Red peppers tumble from the market tables in abundance. I buy a kilo (2 pounds) at a time and use them in sauces, soups, and as a crispy raw salad. I serve these marinated "boats" with their anchovy "sailors" from a pretty lacquered Japanese boat bought at a sushi bar. I remember great anchovies, bought in Cadaques, pickled whole in vinegar and draped over peppers in imitation of the little red Catalan fishing boats like *Julia* that sail from Port Lligat. Sail away!

2 sweet red peppers
12 to 16 anchovy filets
freshly ground pepper to taste
1/2 cup (4 fl oz/120 ml) extra virgin olive oil
4 tablespoons red wine vinegar
1 tablespoon chopped fresh thyme, savory, or tarragon

1. Cut the red peppers lengthwise into thirds or quarters following the natural number of sections in each pepper. Slice each section lengthwise in half. These are the little "boats." Trim off any of the white ribs and remove the seeds.
2. Place an anchovy "sailor" in each boat and secure with a toothpick "mast."
3. Sprinkle each pepper boat with ground pepper and place in a shallow dish.
4. Mix the oil, vinegar, and herbs together and pour gently over the boats.
5. Marinate in the refrigerator overnight or eat right away.
6. Serve on top of slices of toasted country bread.

CORNICHONS...COMME GRAND·MÈRE
A Grandmother's Cornichons
Makes 2 quarts

My friend Claude Pompèle always makes his own cornichons, the tart little pickles that are frequently served with pâtés and *terrines* in France. I perfected the art of the subtle grovel whenever my last jar of bright green vinegary slivers would empty. When he caught my hint, Claude would disappear to the *cave* and return with another full jar. I worried that our fondness for his homemade fare would deplete his own larder.

One July market day at Vianne, when confronted with a wooden box full of the just-picked objects of desire, little green pickles, I saw the solution to my predicament. I would learn to make cornichons, too! It couldn't be that difficult. I asked the young woman under the blue-and-white-striped awning for a kilo of the pickles. As she began to weigh them out, filling a plastic bag full, I confidently added that I would take all of them since so few remained in the box. The furry, inch-long pickles were weighed in handfuls and placed in my basket. As is my habit when learning a new recipe, I asked the young market vendor how she made her cornichons and confided quietly

HERBED SEA SALT

I buy a 10-kilo (22-pound) bag of salt from the cooperative when I visit my friends on the Île de Ré. This is more salt than I'll ever use in a year or two, but I give some to friends, use some to clean my copper pots along with vinegar, and throw a handful or two in my bath when I want to soak my kitchen-weary bones. (On the Île de Ré, one of the charming Atlantic coast islands, they plant a fragrant pink flowering herb around some salt beds so the flower petals fall from the plants and are blown into the pond by the fresh seaweed-laden air to naturally perfume the pale pink salt for bath salts.)

I always make one batch of herbed sea salt using just thyme and salt, since thyme is the herb I have in most abundance in the garden at our canal-side farmhouse. Next, I make a mix of fresh thyme, bay leaf, rosemary, sage, and fennel seeds in proportions according to my whims or whatever is at hand. The freshness of the herbs seems to seep into the damp salt, and together they marry in a glass jar for a few weeks, or for a few minutes if I am already in the middle of cooking something.

Saturday morning

that it was my first time. A puzzled look came over her face, *"Jensaypaw."* (*Je ne sais pas* is French for "I don't know.") Abandoned in my moment of culinary weakness with a kilo-plus of cornichons and nary a recipe in sight, I thought to switch my attention to other market stalls and other recipes. *"Attends,"* she blurted, and disappeared into the crowded market square. I waited as instructed. A minute or two passed. I began to feel a little sheepish at being left holding the bag and "in a pickle," when she returned at a gallop with a gingham-aproned, gray-haired madame in tow. In her still-wet hands, obviously caught at the kitchen sink, she held a giant jar of cornichons! *"Voilà! Ma mère!"*

The pickle vendor's mother began explaining the process for making "cornichons... comme grand-mère" (pickles like grandmother). After she told me twice what I was to do and I repeated the instructions for her, I spotted something in the jar besides the garlic slivers and tarragon she mentioned. *"Kesskesay?"* (*Qu'est-ce que c'est?* is French for "what is that?") I pointed.

"Le petit truc de grand-mère"—Grandmother's little trick, she whispered as she smiled a sly little grin. Popping open the sealed lid, she showed me the 1/2-inch (15 mm) thick lemon slice she uses to hold the pickles beneath the surface of the vinegar—the secret to her citron-perfumed cornichons.

After I had made my first experimental batch, I presented a jar, complete with Madame's special secret, to Claude. *"Mes cornichons...comme grand-mere,"* I announced proudly.

"Whose grandmother?" he teased. Then he spied the lemon slice. *"Qu'est-ce que c'est?*" he puzzled. At last, I had bested Claude. "Let me tell you grand-mère's little trick," I whispered with a smile.

2 lb (1 kilo) cornichons
1 cup coarse sea salt
several sprigs fresh tarragon and thyme
1 bay leaf
4 to 6 cloves garlic, whole and peeled
a small handful whole peppercorns
1 or 2 small hot red peppers
2 to 3 qt (2 to 3 l) white vinegar, enough to cover pickles completely in jars
1/2-inch (15 mm) slice lemon, one for each jar

1. Wash pickles under cold running water, rubbing them briskly with your hands, a few at a time to remove the furry edges.

2. Place pickles in a large colander and sprinkle liberally with coarse salt. Let sit overnight in the sink or over a bowl, as the pickles will "give up" their water.

3. Drain and dry the pickles with a clean dry dishtowel. (Rubbing is preferable to rinsing as some salt remains.)

4. Place pickles in any-sized clean jars with tight-sealing lids. (I found a large barrel jar and made a cork lid to seal it! A good project for your next visit to France; find the perfect cornichon jar!) Place herbs around the pickles, adding slivers of peeled garlic cloves, several peppercorns, and a hot pepper, if desired, per jar.

5. Fill the jars to the top with cold vinegar straight from the bottle.

6. Lay a lemon slice on top and close the lid tight. Shake once or twice and put on the back of a shelf or in the corner of the counter for a week or so. Taste and test the pickles as often as you like. They change in crunch and piquancy as they absorb the brine. They will be done in a month or two if there are any left. Open up a jar of pâté, pour an aperitif, and practice your French. "*Tu veux un cornichon?*"

OIGNONS AU VINAIGRE
Pickled Onions
Makes 1 quart

Once I overcame my fear of putting up things in jars, I was inspired. After a trip to the Italian countryside to visit friends near Cortona, where I loaded up on Italian gastronomic souvenirs, I returned to the *Julia Hoyt* with a bottle of pickled onions in hand. A beautiful pot-bellied glass jar filled with flat white onions (known as *cipolino*) in a pale rose-colored vinegar. I have since found cipollino onions in California, but in France I buy the tiny pearl onions used for boiling and enjoy similar results. I serve these at aperitif time or alongside pâtés and sausages in place of the famous cornichons.

1 lb (500 g) very small onions
4 cups (32 fl oz / 1 liter) cider vinegar
2 tablespoons sugar
12 whole peppercorns
1 cinnamon stick

1. Boil water in a four-quart pan. Plunge the onions in the boiling water for one minute, drain, and rinse under cold water. Peel off the skin, trim the onions, and drain.
2. Bring the vinegar and sugar to a lively simmer over medium-high heat. When sugar is dissolved, after two minutes or so, add the peppercorns and cinnamon and remove from the heat. Let sit five minutes.

3. Place the peeled onions in clean jars and cover with the vinegar mixture and spices. Put lids on and let sit for several days to a month. (I taste and test crunchy onions every few days and enjoyed some that I had prepared for Christmas gifts the day after they were put up! Who said preserving food requires patience?)

PÂTÉ DE POULET
Chicken Pâté
Makes 12 8-ounce jars

Like so many other luxury treats, pâté used to be considered food of the poor. Farmers made pâté because that was what one did with the leftover bits and pieces from butchering a pig or raising the ducks for foie gras. Now we make pâtés because they taste so good! This pâté is made mostly from chicken (stewing hens are best) and is lighter in texture than liver or pork pâtés. I like this tasty version which is made by our friend Claude Pompèle by the kilos. I've adapted the recipe so that we can enjoy just a terrine for a party or have a few jars to put on the pantry shelf. If you want to stock your larder or give some jars as gifts, double the recipe, as Claude does.

4 lb (2 kilos) uncooked chicken meat including the liver and gizzard (a 6 lb (3 kilo)
    stewing hen will yield about 4 pounds of meat)
1 lb (500 g) pork sausage
1 large onion
2 shallots
2 eggs
1/4 cup (2 fl oz/60 ml) armagnac
1/4 teaspoon ground nutmeg
1 tablespoon salt
1 tablespoon freshly ground pepper
several bay leaves

1. Pass through a meat grinder or hand-chop finely the chicken, pork, onions, and shallots.

2. Add the eggs, one half of the armagnac, nutmeg, salt, and pepper and mix well.

3. Starting with clean, sterile canning jars (4 to 8 ounce jars are handy sizes), dip a paper towel in the remaining armagnac and wipe the inside of the jars. Fill with the chicken mixture, patting in the jar as you fill. Top with a bay leaf and seal. Place the jars in a boiling water bath and cook 1 1/2 to 2 hours, depending on the size of the jars.

4. Remove jars from hot water, turn upside down, and let cool. Store in a cool, dark cupboard or pantry. Serve with toast or crackers and cornichons.

Variation

This same recipe can be used to make two terrines to serve for a large party. To cook, preheat an oven to 375 degrees F (190 C). Pat the chicken mixture in two large loaf pans that have been wiped with armagnac. Place a bay leaf on each terrine and cover with a sheet of aluminum foil. Place in a *bain-marie* in the hot oven and cook for 1 1/2 hours. The pâté will shrink some during cooking. Let cool and turn out onto a plate before slicing and serving.

TARTE DE TOMATES MATELOT
The Mate's Tomato Tart
Serves 4 — 6

This is so easy to prepare (especially if you keep a package of pastry crust handy) that even our first-mate, Jhon, whipped up a little something like this one day when Patrick and I had been out visiting a château with our guests. It's been a crew tradition ever since in the bistro-galley.

pastry for a 10-inch (25 cm) tart pan (see recipe, page 82)
Dijon mustard (whole grain adds extra texture)
2 or 3 large ripe tomatoes
2 tablespoons olive oil
2 tablespoons capers
salt and pepper to taste
1 teaspoon fresh thyme, chopped
1 teaspoon fresh chives, chopped

1. Preheat oven to 425 degrees F (220 C).
2. Line a tart pan with pastry. Flute or fold the edges neatly.
3. Brush a thick layer of Dijon mustard across the inside bottom and up the sides of the pastry with a pastry brush, the back of a spoon, or your fingers.
4. Layer slices of perfectly ripe garden tomatoes across the bottom of the pan. Drizzle with a little olive oil (I use some of the oil from my olive jar, page 27), garnish with capers, and sprinkle with salt, fresh herbs (or herbed sea salt, page 33), and pepper.
5. Bake for fifteen to twenty minutes until the pastry is golden and crisp. Slice and serve warm or at room temperature. I sometimes serve this lively tart as an accompaniment to a green salad for a light luncheon.

MOULES ÉCLATÉES
Popped Mussels
Serves 4 — 6

August in Gascony usually means a quick trip to the sea. Summer memories of the Île de Ré explode with each bite of these sweet mussels, fresh from the Atlantic coast. This is a fast souvenir that stays our vacation appetites while the more slow-simmering seafood cooks. On the *Julia Hoyt*, this translates to a colorful, easy to prepare *amuse-bouche* (cocktail snack) while glasses of Floc are being served. Everyone isn't a shellfish fan, but this will satisfy those who are and still let you prepare a non-fishy menu for the whole group!

2 dozen small mussels
1 slice jambon de Bayonne or prosciutto ham
2 shallots, finely chopped
1 clove garlic, minced
1 red pepper, roasted, seeded, and chopped (fresh or from a jar)
1 small bunch parsley, chopped
1 ripe tomato, seeded and chopped (no ripe tomatoes? just leave it out)
hot pepper flakes to taste
3 tablespoons olive oil
3 tablespoons wine vinegar
salt and freshly ground pepper to taste

1. Wash and clean mussels, removing any "beards," and set aside.
2. Combine all other ingredients into a lumpy vinaigrette and let sit together for fifteen minutes. This can be done in advance and stored in the refrigerator. If refrigerated, let mixture come to room temperature before using.
3. Use a cast-iron or other very heavy skillet. The pan must be as hot as a grill without using any oil or fat. You are dry-roasting the mussels. Heat the heavy skillet on high until pan is very hot.

4. Toss in all the mussels and shake gently. They will start to pop open and give their juices to the hot pan within minutes. When all the mussels are open (three to five minutes), add the spicy vinaigrette to the pan and swirl or stir the ingredients into the shells. The addition of the liquids melding with the mussel liquid will open the shells further and the sauce will fill each shell.

5. As soon as the mussels are well coated with the glaze, place on waiting plates and serve with pieces of garlicky toast and very large napkins. Eat with your fingers, using one licked-clean shell as a pair of pincers, and think of brightly painted fishing boats.

BROCHETTES D'AGEN
Prunes and Merguez Sausage Brochettes

Prunes are to Agen as apples are to Normandy, olives to Provence, and walnuts to the Périgord. They are *the* regional fruit and one of the prime agricultural products of the Lot-et-Garonne département of France. Merguez are slim, spicy sausages originally from North Africa and usually made from lamb and flavored and colored with pomegranate juice and peppers. The bite of the spicy-hot sausage complements the sweet jam taste of the prunes as they cook together over the grill. I serve a morsel of each on a toothpick with a pot of strong Dijon mustard for dipping.

6 spicy sausages, merguez or other, cut in 1-inch (3 cm) chunks
1 lb (500 g) pitted prunes
steel or bamboo skewers

1. If using bamboo skewers, soak them in water for thirty minutes before using so they won't burn on the grill.

2. Alternate sausage chunks with the prunes on skewers.

3. Grill over a moderate fire until the sausage is done and the prunes start to caramelize.

4. Serve with a dipping sauce of mustard or other spicy glaze on the side.

MEILHAN·SUR·GARONNE

La Plus Belle Boucherie...

CASTETS
en-DORTHE

écluse 53

écluse 52

écluse 51

BASSANNE
*écluse 50
Bassanne*

LA REOLE
(toutes resources)

écluse Fontet 49
FONTET

train station

HURE
*Epicerie ·
turning spot ·*

48 écluse L'Auriole

♡ Boucherie

MEILHAN
(toutes resources)

*Gironde
Lot-et-Garonne*

MEILHAN-SUR-GARONNE is a quiet day's journey by barge on the canal from Castets-en-Dorthe. We could drive in just twenty-five minutes in our nine-passenger van what takes seven hours on the *Julia Hoyt*. Except in the bistro-galley, speed doesn't count on a barge; the slower we go, the more we see. I notice the stone *bornes* (milestones) passing alongside the narrow road that follows the canal, announcing the hamlets and villages and the kilometers lying between. D-9, Fontet, six kilometers.

At first, it's hard to get your tongue around the names of the villages in this part of France. (Almost as hard as maneuvering the *Julia Hoyt* into the first locks of the day.) They don't sound quite French and all of the letters are pronounced, most of the time. We pass the little communities of Bassanne, Fontet, and Hure, which welcome us at bends in the canal between stretches of wild blackberry jungle and well-groomed fields of ever-growing corn. Although not located on the Garonne River, these simple country villages of church, shops, cafe, and houses have adapted to the canal as if it were their own river and had always been there.

I'm certain that geography and commerce dictated that the canal would pass here and bypass there, but an artist's eye was at work as well. Why else would the nineteenth-century canal widen into a reflecting pond at Fontet, mirroring its twelfth-century château chapel? This romanesque stone landmark, with its

PP. 1323-2. - HURE (Gironde) — Le Bourg

Latapy, édit.

Meilhan (L. et G.) - Vue Générale

1. - FONTET (Gironde) - Le Pont du Canal M. D.

Souvenirs of the long village

43

bell facade carved in simple hearts and built 700 years before the canal, still rings the Angelus and is a favorite Sunday rendezvous for fishermen and families. It is for me a classic landscape portrait of my long village. A wild plum tree grows nearby and when we stop for a lunch or a moonlit evening mooring here, the crew disappear with baskets in hand and return with juice dripping between the reeds. A simple tart or impromptu jam of these *prunes de cochon*—pig's plums—is the reward.

On the way to Meilhan, we stop at one of my favorite old villages, Hure. Stretching along a wide bend of evenly spaced plane trees, Hure is a perfect curve of deep shade that seems to draw us into the quiet of life in these small rural villages, strung along the canal like so many medieval pearls on a silver chain. The old mill at the Écluse de l'Auriole announces the approach to Hure, a nearly unpronounceable village. Somewhere between a cough and purr, I can never quite get it right, so I usually refer to "that village just after Fontet" rather than make an unsuccessful attempt to mimic how the natives say "Hure," as "*Uuorrra.*"

Hure is one of my secret, special places. Special because of the Roman mosaics, a souvenir of another world, hidden within the medieval church.

Secret because the things that I like about Hure are almost insignificant: the *boulangerie* sign with the cartoon baker, the little house with a massive climbing yellow rose, a handpainted sign that reads *"bien faire—bien dire,"* the rows of geraniums placed in pots along a stretch of sidewalk, an open barn door in the middle of town that revealed a half-dozen black-and-white cows one morning, and especially the little all-under-one-roof grocery store. This *épicerie* (grocery) sells lettuce and eggs, bread and croissants, flower pots, garden hats, slippers, and *sabots* (wooden shoes). People around here still wear sabots to work in the wet gardens and keep their feet dry. Sometimes I stop and buy butter or pick up an extra liter of milk in this modest shop just so I can overhear the rolling village conversations and sing a five-note *"bonjour, messieurs-dames"* to everyone in the store. Although it is not a tourist destination, I stop at Hure because I believe it is in the ordinary daily events in this rural countryside that the most extraordinarily romantic things happen. I buy a blue housedress and wooden shoes to wear in my garden at Camont.

Meilhan-sur-Garonne sits up high above a grand horseshoe bend of La Garonne and its canal port. This is our mooring for our second night, silent between owl calls. From La Tertre, the site of a pre-Roman mound where a restaurant now replaces a temple, one can overlook the canal, the river, and the broad plains of the intensively farmed valley. Like Castets, Meilhan is a double village; there is the village on high and the canal- and river-hugging village

below. The hand-stenciled sign approaching the steep road that connects the two halves informs travelers and reminds residents that this is *un beau village de France.* This beautiful village in France is home to the sleepy baker who never opens until 8 o'clock but would invite me in to hear the hot, crackling baguettes "singing" in the flour-dusted air. *"Écoute, elles chantent."*

I am always eager, as the *Julia Hoyt* slips in between the house-

The approach to Hure

barges *Tage* and *Maja*, to dash up the long hill to the village top before the shops close. A favorite is The Butcher. Locals, too, refer to this *boucherie* with reverence in their tone. Nowhere else along the canal do I crave the aromas of roasting meats, stewing shanks, and grilling sausage as much as at Meilhan.

I climb a footpath from the canal bridge and ascend to the top of town. Although no sign proclaims it, in my view this is one of the *plus belle boucheries de France*. The trademark red leather waiting bench is usually occupied. Red has always been associated with butcher shops in France, the color of the *abattoir* (the slaughterhouse), the aprons, the meat trays. Now, weather-stained "for sale" signs tacked to faded red storefronts announce that the *hypermarché* (supermarket) plague threatens village life. The red tile, the ancient meat hooks, the tattered crimson awnings or painted carmine *boiserie* (wooden facade) visible in every village hint at a past of freshly slaughtered carcasses and whole haunches hanging.

It took several visits to Boucherie Laurans before I realized what good fortune I had encountered on my first irregular shopping expedition and what The Red Bench, worn smooth by countless villagers, signified. With my mental list for dinner at hand, I entered the shop and glanced at the tiled walls. A large, neatly printed panel proclaims that the veal is from Monsieur Duthoron, the beef from Chez Carbonnet, the poultry the grace of Madame Dusseaux, and the sausages are *fait maison*, made in the shop. I had never before seen such pride and admission of ownership about a rump roast or a leg of lamb! The plump rabbit and the guinea hen are as prized as the top livestock from 4-H fairs at home.

Waiting my turn, I began an impromptu revision of the week's dinner list. Look at those saucisses de Toulouse! Perfect for grilling and serving with little green lentils, the *lentilles du Puy*. The *jarret de veau* would make a simple dinner after wine tasting and that fat yellow-skinned stewing hen will become Vetou's *poule au pot*. I turned recipes over in my head and rearranged menus as I began to understand snatches of conversation. The same process was being repeated between housewife and cook around the room and on The Red Bench near me.

My turn approached as the next local resident moved to the counter. "*Eh, Monsieur Barthe*, what will it be today?" Barely tall enough to see over the glass and chrome counter to the waiting butcher in his one-shoulder apron, Monsieur Barthe was dressed in the ubiquitous "working blue" *serge de Nîmes* (denim to us) uniform of farmer and artisan, beret placed squarely on his head, well-used shopping basket set between his rubber-shoe-clad feet. Old Monsieur Barthe began a soliloquy of meat the likes of which I had never heard before.

"Give me that *jarret* of veal. *Oui*, the whole piece, the three kilos! Of course leave the bone in! *Non*, of course, it's not too much. And a thick slice of *entrecôte*. Make it thicker, my boy. Now, wrap up some *saucisses* for me. The plump ones. Six, ten, no, make it a fat dozen. And I'll have some liver. Liver of lamb, not mutton, and place two kidneys in with the package."

My eyes widened as I pictured the fantastic feast that this unlikely cook was going to produce for an elbow-worn table of old men in berets.

Even when his purchases were freshly wrapped in white paper with a picture of the canal and river, tied with string and bagged, paid for, and basketed, I was still calculating the kilos of meat that he was carting home when I overheard one elderly woman whisper to the other, "*Quel vieux garçon!*" (What an old bachelor!) I sank in the realization that rather than an exceptional Sunday dinner for twelve old bereted men, elbows on table and knives in hand, our old Monsieur Barthe was shopping for the entire week, as were all the others waiting in line for service on the busy Saturday morning.

The red leather bench slowly rotated and when a place on it emptied, I settled in for a forty-five-minute wait until time for my small request. "A *bifteck* from the Blondes of Aquitaine on Monsieur Sabadini's farm. I'd like that large rabbit in the back, please. Have you any lamb *côtelettes*? Good, I'll take eight. Wrap up some merguez sausage, please, six, ten, no, a dozen...and a ham bone for some soup." In my long village this is a welcome stop to restock the larder with roasts, chops, sausages, smoked bacon, and a fresh hen for good measure.

SOUP

In explaining the ever-present soup course in Gascony, Vetou Pompèle shrugged her shoulders and said, *"On soupait beaucoup ici."* (We soup a lot here.) A meal always begins with a soup (following aperitifs, of course!). I began to mimic my French friends and start my meals on the *Julia Hoyt* with a simple soup. The soup would be a preview of the rest of the meal, a prelude to the style and flavors to follow.

I began to think in terms of introductions, and attention-getting devices like in the theater where three knocks sounded before the curtain rose in old French comedies. The soup became the theatrical device that heralds the start of the meal and sets the senses on edge as fragrances drift up to the front deck. How scene-setting to bring a mysterious covered tureen to the table, then steam the salon windows when the lid is raised. Or parade an antique two-handled bowl of golden cream to the foredeck to focus the diners from sunset to table.

But in this rustic countryside, soup was the whole meal for many generations. Fava beans and onions were the foundation of country soups and are still recalled in the *garbure* (cabbage and bean stew) and hearty *soupe aux fèves* (fava bean soup) bubbling in ancient toupins on the back of Gascon stoves. Until quite recently, soup was always served for breakfast in the country with thick slices of *pain de campagne*, country bread, soaking in the bottom of a shallow bowl. I imagine even now on winter mornings if you peeked between the faded green shutters of village and country homes, you might still see heads bent over breakfast soup bowls.

The word "soup" originally meant just the pieces of bread soaked in meat juice when the custom was introduced by the Frank king, Mérovée, in the fifth century. Now, as then, in Gascony most country soups are thickened by placing slices of yesterday's bread, often rubbed with garlic, in the tureen or bowls. Occasionally, short pieces of fine pasta or *perles du Japon* (tapioca) are added to give body to a light broth. In the deep country of my adopted heartland, they even "stuff" soup. A *farci* (stuffing) is prepared of beaten eggs, ham, herbs, and bread, and cooked like an omelet until it can just hold its shape. It is then slipped gently onto the top of a simmering soupe aux fèves and steamed by the broth before it is served with pickled cornichons. A local proverb says that the person who cuts the farci in the family is the one who "wears the pants."

Learning to make soup in the southwest of France was like learning my times tables; shallots times garlic, thyme times a bay leaf. Over and over again. The first lists of ingredients stood apart one by one, then faster and faster, as I began to see the connections and multiply the simple base ingredients times whatever produce was available. Always a little fat, duck fat preferred, a chopped onion and garlic, a potato or two to thicken, and salt, pepper, and seasonings.

The French know well the chemistry that takes place as a shallow plate of herb-perfumed broth is passed along the table and the alchemy of spoon and soup makes magic. Even in summer, menus on the *Julia Hoyt* are filled with soups. Not the slow-cooking, long-winter-days hearty soups like garbures and other variations on bean stews but the one-note soups of vegetables and broth, the quick *tourins* of garlic, onion, and egg, and the surprising appetite-quickening herbal broth creams that jump from garden to table in less than thirty minutes. I rarely use a meat or poultry stock since refrigerator space in the bistro-galley is delicately fought over on a daily basis. But I always use good water. Old Monsieur Dupuy says that good water makes good soup. He treks each day with his jug on his cane to fetch clear pure spring water for his soup. Think about this before you turn on your chemical-scented taps, and reach instead for a bottle of clear spring water when making soup!

Farmyard dovecote

Since my schedule on the *Julia Hoyt* prohibits me from hours at the stove, slowly simmering a rich stock, I have developed these soups as "fast food." The lighter vegetable-based soups are fast and elegant and set the mood for lunches and dinners. I discovered the ease of using fresh garden vegetables, a handful of aromatic herbs and spices, and some foraged wild greens to get the gastronomic attention of cast and crew. In the fall, I use a slab of bright orange *potiron* (pumpkin) for a harvest soup; in spring, violet asparagus too irregular to be ribboned into perfectly tied bunches is puréed with cream. Red tomatoes in August, purple artichokes in May, mushrooms in golden October...these rainbow pots are a prelude to a typical Gascon meal, as prescribed by the home cooks who taught me. Knock. Knock. Knock.

Tourin d'Ail
Garlic Soup
Serves 4—6

In Gascony, this fortifying soup is traditionally served to newlyweds on their wedding night. Delivered in a new chamber pot to the bedroom by prankster friends long after midnight, the eggs, garlic, pepper, and vinegar serve as rustic aphrodisiacs. One late evening in May as a pair of newlyweds prepared for bed while honeymooning on the *Julia Hoyt*, our French friends arrived with this soup to fete the young Americans. Since then, I often make this soup just so we can tell the stories of romance on the canal. This is a highly aromatic soup to star in or start a meal and because there is no stock involved, it is a perfectly simple and fast soup to prepare from the pantry.

1 teaspoon duck fat or butter
1 whole head garlic, peeled and crushed

1 yellow or white onion, chopped
4 shallots, chopped
1 tablespoon all-purpose flour
salt and freshly ground pepper to taste
3 egg yolks
1 tablespoon wine vinegar
4 to 6 toasted bread slices, one for each bowl

1. In a 2-quart (2 liter) saucepan, bring 1 1/2 quarts (1.5 liters) of water to boil. Meanwhile, put the fat in a sauté pan over medium-low heat. Add the chopped garlic, onion, and shallots and let them begin to "sweat." Stir the mixture often as the garlicky bits begin to soften, taking care to turn down the heat if they start to brown.

2. Sprinkle with the flour and stir. Cook slowly a little longer, but remove from heat before the vegetables begin to color.

3. Add salt and pepper to the boiling water, then add the vegetable mixture and simmer for about twenty minutes to infuse like a strong tea. When the garlic has given all its flavor to the soup broth and the garlic cloves are very soft, purée with a hand mixer in the pot or transfer to a blender, purée, and then return to the pot.

4. Beat the egg yolks in a small dish with the vinegar. After adding a few tablespoons of the hot soup to the egg yolks, whisk the egg/vinegar mixture into the hot soup and stir over medium heat until the soup just starts to look creamy. Do not boil or the egg will curdle.

5. Adjust the seasoning (we like it quite peppery and I will often add more vinegar at this time). Present the soup ladled over toasted bread that has been placed in individual bowls or a tureen.

LITTLE RADISH SANDWICHES

As Americans eat peanut butter sandwiches, French children and adults eat radish sandwiches. Radishes, butter, and salt are a perfect summer appetizer. I find that most Americans are afraid of the rawness of the

presentation, which is what I love best: a ramekin of sweet butter, piles of salt and freshly ground pepper side by side, and a bunch of red round radishes tied like a nosegay. For the uninitiated, I spread the butter on slices of baguettes, slice a radish into a little fan, sprinkle with salt and pepper, and arrange on a platter.

SOUPE AUX FANES DE RADIS
Radish Leaf Soup
Serves 4—6

"*Eh, voilà*, with just four francs, you make a soup and still have the radishes to eat with bread and butter. A real *paysanne* feast!" The market vendor holds up the peppery red globes bound like a nosegay with a little ribbon like those used to tie tomato plants. Their tops are fresh, bright green, and peppery, too. Radish Leaf Soup is as green as watercress and just as pungent. This can be an almost instant soup as you unpack the market baskets and serve with some great dried sausage, rustic bread, and radishes and butter, of course!

1 bunch firm red radishes, with fresh, bright-green leaves
1 1/2 teaspoons sweet butter
1 onion, chopped finely
3 cloves garlic, crushed
salt and fresh ground pepper, to taste
sprinkle freshly ground nutmeg
2 potatoes, peeled and chopped

1. Take the fresh and pungent bunch of radishes and twist the radishes off their leaves. Set the radishes aside for eating separately. Wash the leaves well under running water and drain.

2. Melt butter. Place onion in a 2-quart soup pan as the butter is melting. Add garlic and slowly sauté.

3. After shaking off the excess water, add the whole radish leaves to the onion/garlic mixture. Cook until wilted for a few minutes, then add 1 quart (1 liter) hot water.

4. As it comes to a boil, season with salt, pepper, and nutmeg over medium heat.

5. Add the potatoes and cook fifteen to twenty minutes. When potatoes are soft, purée soup with a hand mixer, a blender, or a food mill. Toast thin slices of bread in goose fat in a heavy skillet and serve right away.

Variation

This very green soup can be made with watercress, nettles, or other tender greens. If you use nettle tips, pick them in the spring as the young shoots arrive. Gather nettles with care (and gloves!). Plunge them into boiling water for one minute, then drain and rinse under cold water. This will remove the formic acid that puts the sting in stinging nettles. It's worth the effort for the surprised look on your guests' faces, as well as for its flavor.

Soupe aux Poireaux Ma Façon
Leek Soup Vinaigrette
Serves 4

This soup is a variation on leeks vinaigrette, a popular starter in bistros, cafes—
and canal barges. I serve it hot as is or iced down and cold with the addition of a
little crème fraîche. The classic combination of leeks and a mustardy vinaigrette
is always welcomed at the bistro-galley on the *Julia Hoyt*. This recipe can be
made without the oil for a totally fat-free soup.

4 to 6 medium-sized leeks
2 medium potatoes, peeled and chopped or diced
1 large shallot
1 bunch fresh chives, chopped
2 teaspoons mustard
2 tablespoons vinegar
2 tablespoons extra virgin olive oil
salt and freshly ground pepper, to taste

1. Clean and trim the leeks. Trim off the roots and most of the dark green
tops; save the tops for stock or other soups. This gritty job is done nicely under
running water or by slicing the leeks into thin rounds first, throwing them into
a pot, and running it full of cold water. The turbulence of the running water
will help remove any sand and you can then scoop out the clean-sliced leeks as
they float on top of the water.

2. Put leeks and potatoes in a 3-quart pot. Cover with 1 quart of water, bring
to a boil, then lower to medium heat and cook until tender, about fifteen minutes.

3. Add shallot and most of the chives and simmer five minutes more.

4. Remove from heat. Potatoes and leeks should be soft, and chives will still
be bright green. Use a hand mixer to purée the soup in the pan, or use a food
mill, blender, or food processor for the job. The potatoes and the bulk of the
leeks are enough to thicken the soup without adding cream or eggs.

5. Make the vinaigrette with the mustard, vinegar, and one tablespoon of the
oil. Salt and pepper to taste. Stir the vinaigrette into the soup. After ladling into
bowls or a tureen drizzle remaining tablespoon of olive oil on the surface.
Garnish with remaining chives.

SOUPE AUX DEUX CÉLERIS
Two-Celery Soup
Serves 4

Celery root is easy to find in abundance in France. The solid round root is featured raw as crudités, or cooked, puréed, and gratinéed. Look for the large, heavy roots in supermarkets and greengrocers. The nutty celery flavor and the firm white meat sweeten as it slowly cooks. I often feature it with its branch cousin, celery hearts, in stews and other soup. This is a tasty introduction to a roast pork dinner.

1 large celery root
1 small bunch celery, including the heart and a few leaves from the top
2 to 3 shallots, peeled and chopped coarsely
2 oz ventreche, pancetta, or unsmoked bacon, diced
1 teaspoon duck fat or butter
salt and freshly ground pepper, to taste
2 tablespoons crème fraîche
freshly ground nutmeg

1. Peel and chop the celery root into large chunks and coarsely chop the celery stalks. Set aside.

2. Place shallots, meat, and duck fat in a heavy-bottomed 3-quart saucepan over medium heat.

3. Stir the shallots and meat until lightly brown; remove and set aside. Toss in all of the celery and stir until coated with the little fat from the meat. Salt and pepper well and cover with 1 quart water.

4. Let the soup come to a boil, then turn heat down and cook until the celery pieces are soft.

5. Remove from heat. Purée with a hand mixer or leave coarse as is. Swirl in a dollop of crème fraîche. Serve the soup topped with the shallots and bacon. Dust with a generous cracking of fresh pepper and ground nutmeg on top and a sprig of celery leaves to garnish.

POTAGE DE JARDIN AUX HERBES
Herb Garden Soup

This simple light cream soup starts with a walk to the herb pots on the deck of the boat with my scissors in hand, and finishes as an elegant aromatic cream. It only takes a few minutes to prepare and is a nice prelude to the herb-influenced Lapin au Cresson. Use only the freshest herbs and infuse them gently in the soup.

1 teaspoon butter
1 medium onion, chopped
1 shallot, chopped
mixed fresh herbs—thyme, sage, chives, hyssop, and rosemary or whatever is available (use only tender leaves and remove any woody stems.)
1 egg yolk
1/2 cup (4 fl oz/125 ml) crème fraîche or fresh liquid cream
salt and freshly ground white pepper, to taste

1. Melt the butter in a 3-quart saucepan. Add the onion and shallot and let soften over medium heat. Add 1 quart of water and the herbs, and let simmer slowly for fifteen minutes.

2. Remove from heat and purée the herbs and onion in the pan with a hand mixer or in a blender.

3. Stir the beaten egg yolk into the cream and add to soup a little at a time.

4. Add salt and white pepper and stir over medium heat until slightly thickened. Serve in small bowls with a garnish of fresh herbs and garlic croutons.

GARLIC CROUTONS
While the soup is simmmering, I take a few bread slices, rub them with a garlic clove cut in half, cut the slices in irregular pieces, drizzle them with olive oil, and salt and pepper them. Toss the seasoned bread chunks in a hot frying pan or in a hot oven on a baking sheet and toast until golden brown.

LOCKHOUSES AND THE LOCKKEEPERS

The twenty-one *écluses* in my long village all have names. "Gravières," "Bernes," and "L'Avance" are the three écluses we pass after leaving the last village, Meilhan. Locks are the stairsteps in our long canal system as we move from sea level up to 600 feet near Castelnaudary on the Canal du Midi and back down to sea level at the Mediterranean Sea. Sometimes there are miles between locks, other times just yards as we climb to cross an obstacle like a river or jump a small stream.

The little lockhouses are painted yellow with green shutters and they all have red-tiled roofs. Like toy houses in a children's game, each one is almost the same; a garden here, a laundry line there, a pile of wood stacked for the winter. In the old days, there were always contests for the best lockhouse gardens.

Most locks on the Latéral are automatic now and few lockkeepers are needed to control the hydraulic works. But the remaining lockkeepers still play an important role. Connected by a handcrank field telephone, they spread the word that the péniche *Julia* is on the way. If a commercial barge is around the next bend, the lock-keeper we've dubbed "Columbo" because of his likeness to the television character, warns us to keep our heads up for *Barran*, who is riding high and empty and can't see over his bow. The *Mark Twain II* leaves a message for us to meet the crew for aperitifs. The lockkeepers offer the weather reports, the latest news on canal repairs, and sometimes a coveted recipe from the lockhouse kitchen.

It was the last lockkeeper at the flower-filled Écluse de Gravières who inspired me to start my garden at Camont, our canal-side farmhouse. Each time the *Julia Hoyt* would arrive at Gravières, the lock just after Meilhan, "Madame l'Éclusière" would appear, smiling, to take our lines and pass a word or two of greeting. Each time, on a crooked little bench in front of the green control cabin, a bowl of toma-toes would be waiting, just picked from her garden. There would be a small piece of paper reading "five francs" tucked in among the fat, ripe, crimson-colored balls. I would pass over my basket, we'd exchange coins, the lock gates would open, she'd hand us our lines, and off we'd go.

Last year, when the lockkeeper retired after twenty-five years, we lost more than a friend. Now, the lockhouse sits empty, the garden is abandoned, and the little vegetable stand is gone.

Soupe d'Été aux Melons et Verveine
Summer Soup with Melons and Lemon Verbena
Serves 4

Verveine (lemon verbena) is one of the most fragrant plants surviving from year to year in my canal-side herb garden at Camont. A cross between a bush and a tree, its long, narrow leaves, bright green and textured, give off their heady, lemony perfume when raked with a fingernail. At summer's end, I spread lemon verbena branches among the napery to scent the freshly washed cottons, damasks, and linens as we put them away for the winter. Branches are tucked in the bedsheets and towels, too. But it is the leaf that is most often used in desserts or to flavor ancient brandy recipes. Lemon verbena is sometimes used in place of mint, as I have used it in this adaptation of Maria-Claude Gracia's *soupe au melon*, a fragrant, not quite sweet soup served when the markets overflow with mountains of ripe melons. Locally these softball-sized, smooth-skinned globes are called *melons de Nerac* because they come from the nearby hills of Nerac. Heavy with juice and orange-fleshed like a cantaloupe, they are harvested from vast fields and brought directly to market in large wooden flats on the back of tractors. Choose your melon by weight and smell. The heavier and more fragrant, the better.

1 very ripe melon; any soft-fleshed and heavily-scented summer melon will do
4 leaves fresh or dried lemon verbena (available dried as a tea)
1 tablespoon butter
1 white onion, minced
salt and white pepper to taste
1 tablespoon vanilla vinegar (see Ingredients List)

1. Cut the melon in quarters, then cut the flesh in pieces, eliminating the rind, fibers, and seeds. Place the pieces of melon in a pot with 1 quart (1 liter) of water and the lemon verbena leaves. Bring to a simmer over medium heat for twenty minutes.

2. Melt the butter in a 2-quart (2-liter) pan over low heat. Add the onion and cook gently until it is very soft and translucent.

3. Add the melon and its liquid and stir. Add salt and pepper to taste and let come to a quick boil. Remove from heat.

4. Leave as is or purée with a hand mixer, blender, or food processor. Before serving, stir in a tablespoon of vanilla vinegar to heighten the taste. A squeeze of fresh lemon juice could be used instead, but I like the way the vanilla-scented vinegar complements the melon and lemon verbena. This can also be chilled and served cold.

A Truckstop Menu

Along the canal-side roads we sometimes moor at a *routier,* a truckstop or workman's cafe, and learn what the local plumbers, plasterers, or stonemasons eat for lunch. In these local canteens at linen-covered tables, forty to fifty workingmen munch on first courses of soup followed by quiche and crudités, eat duck breast in green peppercorn sauce, and plow through salads and cheese, fruit, and dessert before a final *petit café.* I have become used to the sight of these informal gatherings, where newcomers join the tables until they are filled and people pass the bottles of wine and pitchers of water from one to another. The family-style service always starts with a tureen of soup that is passed from hand to hand and then followed by a cart or tray of heaps of olives, grated celery root and carrots, herring, potato salad, marinated mushrooms, and the like.

In village homes they eat a full lunch, too, when the family gathers around the kitchen table. Lunches last a full two hours. These midday breaks between work lower stress levels and replenish the spirit as well as the stomach. This is what they might eat:

Tomato and Egg Tourin
Pâté and a Terrine
Marinated Wild Mushrooms
Veal in Tomato Sauce with Pasta
Endive Salad
Coffee and Merveilles (doughnut-
     like cakes)

TOURIN DU BATELIER
A Bargeman's Soup
Serves 4 — 6

Living on the *Julia Hoyt*, lunches can be for two, four, or twenty...I remember the summer lunch on the towpath when Colette and Phillipe of the *Mosan* were moored near us. We were enjoying an impromptu lunch of *soupe des tomates* together when the *Kalimiki* sailed up with Maurice and Maïte for a visit. Friends arriving by boat is not an everyday occurrence! We had no sooner enlarged the table from four to six than Maurice shouted, *"Regarde! Des Suisses arrivent avec une vache!"* (Look! The Swiss are coming with a cow!) "The Swiss" were friends of Maurice and Maïte's and cruising on their own little barge-boat, and they were indeed coming upstream in our direction with a bellowing cow keeping pace along the towpath. While we hastily cleared the table out of the way of the much-perturbed galloping beast, I added a few more tomatoes to the soup pot, then called the Sabadinis at the farm at the top of the road. After a detour through our garden at Camont, the big Blonde of Aquitaine heifer finally started up the road to her escaped pasture just as Monsieur Sabadini's tractor arrived.

This tomato, garlic, and egg soup is the recipe that Maurice gave me that day, one that bargemen of the Garonne often made on their quick visits to the galley. Fast, easy, fortifying, and tasty, it is the stuff that legends are made of on hot summer days. When the tomatoes are so ripe that you don't even need to plunge them in boiling water to peel them, that's when you make this soup. How many cows were there? Were there eight people or eighteen? How much pepper did you use?

4 lb (2 kilos) very ripe summer tomatoes, peeled and crushed
2 onions, coarsely chopped
1 handful garlic cloves (4 to 8, depending on your taste), peeled and crushed
salt and freshly ground pepper
2 eggs
fresh chopped basil and thyme, or herbed sea salt (see recipe, page 33)
4 to 6 thick slices country bread rubbed with fresh garlic

1. Place tomatoes into a big pot over medium heat. Add onions and garlic.

2. Add water (about the same volume as the tomatoes) and a generous amount of salt and pepper. Simmer for fifteen minutes, then bring to a gentle boil.

3. Beat the eggs quickly and stir them into the hot soup. Turn the heat down immediately and add the herbs. The herbs will infuse the soup as the eggs cook and thicken this simple tourin.

4. Toast some slices of rustic bread, rub with garlic, and place in a tureen. Pour the soup over the bread. Or serve in bowls with a crusty loaf of bread, a salad, and a bottle of good red wine.

Faux Garbure de Gascogne
Cabbage and White Bean Soup

The nearly singular exception to the light potage as a first course is the area's famous thick garbure—cabbage, bean, and confit stew. This version is called Faux Garbure because I leave out the confit of duck or goose and make do with a few thick slices of *ventreche*, pancetta, salt pork, or ham. The addition of a little slightly rancid duck fat or the very end of a ham on the bone as it reaches its sweet peak of going over is the distinctive flavorful essence necessary to make a very good garbure.

This soup is thick with melting pieces of tender cabbage and the root vegetables of early fall. There is no exact right number of turnips, carrots, or onions. Use what you like. Remember, this soup was traditionally made from what was on hand. Stir in the vegetables with care, and it will show. In Gascony, a garbure would be cooked over the fire, the smell of woodsmoke mingling with the vegetables, and then eaten in the kitchen around the table before the *cheminée*. When a leg or two of duck confit is added, a garbure can become a whole meal.

On the *Julia Hoyt*, this is a dish for a rainy day in the fall when the cribbage games are hot and heavy, Django Rinehardt is playing gypsy music, and the single drip through the galley hatch reminds us that we are safe and warm, somewhere in southwestern France. I think of this as the first cold autumn day's welcome.

1 whole savoy cabbage
1 thick slice ventreche (about 4 oz / 100 g)—pancetta, a ham bone, or a slice of salt pork can be used
2 onions, chopped
1 cup white beans (if using dried beans, soak for 1 hour)
3 cloves garlic, crushed
2 each leeks, carrots, and turnips, peeled and chopped in large pieces
3 to 4 potatoes, peeled and cubed
fresh thyme
1 bay leaf
freshly ground pepper, to taste
1 tablespoon duck fat or olive oil
6 thick slices country bread rubbed with garlic cloves

1. While bringing a pot of water to boil, trim and quarter the cabbage, discarding the core. Blanch the cabbage quarters in the boiling water for five minutes. Remove and drain. Discard the cabbage water.

2. Place the meat, salt pork, or ham bone, one-half of the chopped onion, beans, and about 3 quarts (3 liters) cold water in another pot over medium-high heat. Cook for forty-five minutes to one hour.

3. Add garlic and all the vegetables, except the cabbage, to the simmering beans. Add the thyme, bay leaf, and pepper, and continue simmering. (Salt will probably not be needed since the ventreche or ham is salty enough. Correct seasoning as needed.) Cover and let simmer slowly for thirty minutes.

4. Slice the cabbage quarters into thick slices and add to the soup, stirring in gently to keep the vegetables intact. Let cook very slowly for another hour or so.

5. Take the remaining onion and sauté in the duck fat or oil in a hot pan until well-browned and starting to caramelize. Add to the soup just before serving. If you have a spare leg of duck or goose confit around, by all means, add it in!

6. Prepare a soup tureen by lining it with slices of bread rubbed with garlic. Pour soup over the bread and serve hot with cornichons and ground pepper to pass around.

MARMANDE·LA·JOLIE
To Market, To Market...

IT'S MARKET DAY three times a week in Marmande-la-Jolie, one of the pretty market towns along the Garonne River. A dramatic history of medieval battles and massacres lies beneath the civilized veneer of more recent centuries. Now, Marmande is famous for its fields of bright red tomatoes and sweet *Gariguette* strawberries. Its busy shops and cafes surround the glass-covered market square animated with vendors, shoppers, and browsers.

The bistro-galley is insatiable, like a 65-ton pet waiting to be fed. We leave the boat at Pont des Sables and drive to Marmande. I go to market in one town or another every other day to stock up on fresh produce and search for new treats. I always bring a strong friend along to help carry the heavy baskets. Two baskets are needed: one solid, woven gypsy-made reed basket for the fragile produce and one soft, stringy net basket for the heavy goods such as potatoes and melons. Going to market is also deeply satisfying as the next closest way to get to the source of our food. Who I buy from is almost as important as what I buy.

First, I take a leisurely stroll around the market square. It's Saturday and there are over 100 vendors. I check the lay of the land before I start buying. Where are the lettuce growers that I will buy from last so the fragile greens won't get bruised? Where

*Au marché: Garlic-roasted quail
and white asparagus*

are the old gardeners wearing bow ties or hand-knit sweaters and small-holding farmers with three baskets of shallots, two jars of jam, and one dozen eggs? Who has the plumpest ducklings? Who has fresh foie gras? And all the time, I am looking out for the unusual, seasonal items that will change tonight's menu. Small things like *aillets*—tender wild garlic shoots available only in spring—some already shelled tender *fèves* (fava beans) to braise for a side dish with lamb, or the newly uncovered *trompettes de la mort* (poor man's truffles) for an autumn omelet. This first survey is where I'll choose the fresh tuna for a *salade niçoise* or appraise the creamy-blond fresh foie gras to sauté with a syrupy fruit vinegar.

Each market is different in character from place to place and season to season. The thumb-thick white asparagus of May is talked about for eleven months; the first *fraises de bois* (wild strawberries) are only memories until June appears. In July, there are tables heaped with nothing but sweet, smooth-skinned melons. In November, at the market in Casteljaloux, I find the near legendary *broutes* (cabbage shoots) and the best *boudin noir* (black sausage) I've ever tasted. At Nerac, there are roasting quail for a 10:00 a.m. *casse-croûte* (midmorning snack) and paper-covered tables of fresh goat cheese.

In Marmande, I find the fruit for confitures, jars of many-colored honeys, and a cache of coriander, mint, and spices from a North African family. Staples start to fill the baskets. *Aubergines* (eggplants) to roast, tomatoes for stuffing, leeks for soup, new potatoes as small as marbles to roll around in a hot garlicky pan.

Fruit ready to burst its skin is arranged in wooden flats. We take a full four kilos of perfumed white peaches to eat for breakfast, lunch, and dinner. In late summer there are plums of every size and color for eating, cooking, drying, and making eau-de-vie. Southwest France is famous for its prune plums, the *pruneaux d'Agen*. Cultivated here since the eleventh century, the "plum date" was brought back by gourmand crusaders and prized for its sweet storage qualities. There are sticky, dark plums by the ton weight arranged by size and degree of humidity; some cooked for twenty-four hours for keeping, some *mi-cuit* (half-cooked) for soaking in armagnac or wine. In fall there are dozens of varieties of apples to shame the lone Delicious variety most often found in supermarkets. I experiment to find the best one for the elusive "perfect" Tarte Tatin or simple armagnac-perfumed *tarte de pommes*.

Soon, the baskets are overflowing with dinner to come, a special bottle of homemade wine vinegar wrapped in *Le Petit Bleu*, the local newspaper, a carafe of *sirop des herbes* for tinting summer drinks, and a jar of peach jam to hide until October when we've forgotten what color the sun was in summer. Heavily laden and overwhelmed by the sensory treats, we rest at a nearby cafe, Le P'tit Crème, and order *grandes crèmes*, large, steaming cups of milky strong coffee, on cool mornings, or *citron pressé* (fresh lemonade) on hot summer days before returning fully charged to the *Julia Hoyt* at Pont des Sables.

ENTRÉES

Going to the market is always an adventure and a chance to modify my plans for the day's menu, usually in the form of an entrée, the first course. In France, an entrée is a starter, a beginning or an entrance to the meal, not the main course. Restaurants use this first course to highlight the creative talents of the chef and turn simple ingredients into culinary fantasies.

A single elegant morsel or an abundant platter can serve as the beginning of a meal. This is a great time to showcase a seasonal vegetable like asparagus, to be eaten alone, wonderfully presented with no distractions. Or a whole platter of tomatoes with shallots and vinegar that will pass around the table twice. A heap of grated beets with walnuts and dressing, trays of classic crudités, a *tourte* (covered pastry shell) with leeks and mushrooms, a tomato tart with a mustard-painted crust, little wild mushroom pies in autumn or spring, artichokes sautéed or stuffed, or zucchini sliced, toasted, and served with a dip. This is also the time to present something special like a terrine of foie gras served with oven-roasted country bread, crayfish swimming in armagnac sauce, spiced sausage stuffed in eggplant, or escargots in the southwest style with red wine, mushrooms, and ham.

In formal dinners there are often several entrées served in succession or all at once. It is traditional in the Gascon countryside to have at least two cooked meats in a meal. In my long village, I learned that serving only one course for a meal is a lesson in poverty. If all you can offer is the makings for a vegetable stew, then reserve the carrots and make a golden soup to whet the appetite of the diner and broil the tomatoes with herbs to serve separately instead of letting them melt and disappear into the stew. Our eating habits in the United States are spare compared to festive French menus and rustic farmhouse fare.

ASPERGES À LA VINAIGRETTE
Asparagus Vinaigrette
Serves 4

Asparagus is a symbol of spring in Southwest France. The freshly gathered stalks are bundled with ribbon or raffia and stand on their evenly cut stems on market tables throughout April and May. After that, just *un bon souvenir* (a pleasant memory) remains of the grass-sweet flesh until the next year.

Asparagus is usually served with a sharp vinaigrette here in Gascony. These are the large, thumb-sized violet-tipped white asparagus grown in France. In California, asparagus are green and pencil-thin; in Italy, they are deep purple shoots the size of breadsticks. In France, the thick, pale, fleshy shoots are cooked thoroughly after they have been peeled of their tough skins and poached in salted boiling water until easily pierced with a fork through the thickest part of the stalk. In California, asparagus is lightly steamed or boiled so the stalks still snap when bitten. However tender or crispy you like them, this way of serving sets off the almost sweet flavor of the spring's favored food. The highly cherished antique asparagus plates I covet have a well in which to place a sauce or vinaigrette. In simpler country homes, my French friends showed me how to serve

asparagus by placing a fork underneath the top of your plate, tilting the plate gently toward you, and pouring the vinaigrette into the bottom of each plate.

1 bunch fresh asparagus
1 bottle good-quality salad oil—corn, sunflower, or olive oil
1 bottle wine vinegar—red, white, or champagne varieties
salt and freshly ground pepper, to taste

1. Steam or boil the asparagus to your liking. Place on a platter and let cool to room temperature.

2. Pass the oil, vinegar, salt, and pepper around the table. Pour some oil (about 2 tablespoons) and some vinegar (about 1 teaspoon) onto each tilted plate. Sprinkle with salt and pepper.

3. Serve the asparagus. Pick up a piece of asparagus from the platter with your hands and stir the vinaigrette with it a little before popping the tip in your mouth. Continue stirring and eating until you get to the tougher bottom part of the stem. Start over with a new piece, adding more oil and vinegar as needed. Pass finger bowls or damp towels after this entrée!

Asperges de Vetou
Vetou's Asparagus
Serves 4

Sitting around the towpath table, Claude describes the lunch that his wife, Vetou, had prepared that Sunday, including an entrée that is *"hyper bon, incroyable, délicieux."* I agree completely. This is how Vetou prepared asparagus for me the next time I had dinner chez Pompèle.

1 tablespoon duck fat or olive oil
1/2-inch slice (2 oz/60 g) ventreche, pancetta, bacon, or ham, chopped
1 small bunch new spring onions, sliced in half lengthwise
1 small bunch aillets (green garlic shoots), cut in half lengthwise
1 bunch fresh white or green asparagus (about 1 lb/500 g), peeled, trimmed, and
    cut in thirds

1 mint leaf
sprigs of fresh thyme
salt and freshly ground pepper, to taste
1/2 glass white wine or water
1 tablespoon butter, optional

1. Heat the duck fat or olive oil in a heavy, covered sauté pan over medium heat. Add the meat and cook briefly.

2. Add the onions and garlic, sautéing gently until half-cooked. Place the asparagus in the pan. Add mint leaf, a little thyme, and salt and pepper. Cover and cook slowly for ten to fifteen minutes. If the asparagus is fresh, no additional water will need to be added as it gives up its water and makes a delicious sauce at the same time.

3. Add water or wine to the pan and continue cooking without the lid until the asparagus is tender (test with a fork). The wine will marry with the juices to make the sauce.

4. Remove asparagus and onions to a warm serving platter. Reduce the sauce left in the pan by simmering briskly over a high heat until slightly thickened. If you like, stir in butter to enrich the sauce further just as you remove it from the heat. Pour sauce over asparagus and serve hot.

UN, DEUX, TROIS...LES LÉGUMES FARCIS
Three Stuffed Vegetables

Plumped with cooking juices and crowned with golden brown crusts, these three stuffed vegetables are favorites on the *Julia Hoyt*. Eggplants, zucchini, and red peppers are stuffed and served, too. Perfect as an entrée to a meal or to serve as a luncheon dish, stuffed vegetables can also become main courses. A tender young cabbage, when it is stuffed with sausage and poached with vegetables, is dubbed a *poule verte*, a green chicken (See recipe, pages 122-123).

1. TOMATES FARCIES
Stuffed Tomatoes
Serves 4

It is possible to buy stuffed tomatoes in most *charcuteries* or *traiteurs* (delicatessens), but nothing beats the fresh and succulent marriage of sausage, herbs, and tomato juices as this dish emerges hot from the oven and is served as the first course of a hearty meal. These colorful vegetables also make great lunches when served with a salad and some crusty bread, cheese, fruit, and *un petit café*.

4 large ripe tomatoes
1/2 lb (240 g) pork sausage
2 shallots, minced
1 clove garlic, minced
2 tablespoons finely chopped parsley
1 cup (2 oz/50 g) leftover bread
1/4 cup (2 fl oz/60 ml) milk
1 egg
salt and freshly ground pepper, to taste
fresh thyme, sage, and mint (basil and tarragon
   work well, too)
1 tablespoon vegetable oil

1. Preheat oven to 400 degrees F (200 C).

2. Slice the top off each tomato and set aside. Scoop a well from the center of the fruit using a tablespoon. Leave enough meat (about 3/4 inch/2 cm) around the skin so that the tomato holds together.

3. In a bowl, combine the sausage meat, shallots, garlic clove, and parsley.

4. Break up the bread in a little bowl and wet with enough milk so that you can squeeze the pieces like a sponge and the damp mixture holds together easily. Squeeze out excess milk if need be and discard.

5. Beat the egg into the bread mixture and add salt and pepper generously. Season the bread mixture with herbs as desired.

6. Combine the bread mixture with the sausage meat.

7. Stuff the tomatoes with the mixture.

8. Place the tomatoes in a casserole dish that has been brushed with oil. Replace the tomato lids with the help of a toothpick and bake for thirty to forty minutes.

2. ARTICHAUTS À LA MA MÈRE
My Mother's Stuffed Artichokes
Serves 4

It came as a surprise to me to find in the Lot-et-Garonne département of Southwest France a recipe that reminded me of my mother's Italian cooking. It was some time before I learned that many of my French friends are actually of Italian origin. At the same time that my grandfather Giovanni DiPietrantonio arrived in Portland, Maine, from the Abruzzi region of Italy, many other Italian families were arriving in France's Garonne Valley. The farm population was devastated by the losses in World War I. After the war, the French government encouraged immigration into the vast rural countryside. Many of these farms today are run by second- and third-generation Italian settlers who introduced their culinary touch to the region. This recipe turns up in the spring when the local artichokes are abundant and after the first baby chokes have been gathered for sautéing in garlic and oil. My mother always stuffed artichokes just as her mother did. I continue the tradition with this recipe that substitutes the delicious *jambon de pays* (country ham) of Gascony for Italian prosciutto.

4 large artichokes
1/2 fresh lemon
2 cups (4 oz/100 g) leftover bread
1/4 cup (2 fl oz/60 ml) milk
1 egg
salt and freshly ground pepper, to taste
1 onion, finely chopped
1 shallot, finely chopped
1 clove garlic, finely chopped
2 tablespoons olive oil or melted butter
1 slice jambon de pays or prosciutto, diced
1/2 cup (2 oz/60 g) grated Parmesan cheese
1 handful parsley, chopped

1. Preheat oven to 400 degrees F (200 C). Bring a large pot of salted water to boil.

2. Trim the stems off the artichokes. Cut the pointed edges of the leaves off with a pair of scissors. Remove any small, tough bottom leaves. Rub the bottom and the cut edges with the lemon and cook in boiling water until the artichoke heart is just tender, about twenty-five to thirty minutes. (Use a fork to test.) While the artichokes are cooking, prepare the stuffing.

3. Cut the crusts off the bread and, in a mixing bowl, break up the bread into chunks and sprinkle with enough milk to moisten. Squeeze the bread between your fingers and rub well until it becomes mealy and binds together when crushed in your hand. Squeeze, drain, and discard any excess milk. Beat in the egg, salt, and pepper.

4. Place the onion, shallot, and garlic in a hot pan with a little of the oil and start to brown. Add the prosciutto or ham to the browning onion mixture. Let the meat color slightly. Add to the bread mixture.

5. Stir in the Parmesan cheese and chopped parsley and mix the stuffing well.

6. Remove the artichokes from the boiling water and drain upside down. As soon as they are cool enough to handle, spread the leaves gently and work the stuffing in and around the base of each leaf. The artichoke will be plump and each leaf will have a bite of stuffing. Drizzle each choke with some olive oil or melted butter, dust with Parmesan cheese and place in an oven-proof dish. Bake for fifteen to twenty minutes, or until the artichoke stuffing is crispy on the edges and the cheese is melted.

3. OIGNONS FARCIS
Stuffed Onions
Serves 4

These sweet golden globes bursting from the oven are always a favorite on the *Julia Hoyt*. I often serve smaller versions of these stuffed with onion confiture (see recipes, page 139) as an accompaniment for roast fowl or meat. They cook in the oven at the same time as the roast and caramelize the pan juices. I like these stuffed with cheese, bread, and lots of fresh herbs as a first course to let my guests savor the special melting sweetness of the slow-baked onions. I made these for our wedding menu, "The Luncheon of the Boating Party," with Lapin aux Pruneaux, Carrots Glazed with Rosé Wine, and Petits Monets for dessert.

4 medium onions
1 cup (2 oz/50 g) cubed bread chunks (tear into small pieces the size of dice)
1 tablespoon butter
1 cup (4 oz/120 g) grated Gruyère cheese
1 teaspoon orange zest
1 handful raisins
fresh tarragon, parsley, and chives
salt and freshly ground pepper, to taste
2 tablespoons armagnac

1. Preheat oven to 350 degrees F (180 C). Put on a 3-quart pan of water to boil.

2. Slice off the top of each onion and just enough of the root base so that it will sit flat. Do not peel. With a melon baller, scoop out a hollow in the onion. It is easier to do this before the onion is parboiled. Chop reserved onion core to use later.

3. Plunge the onions in their skins into the boiling water and let parboil for ten minutes. Drain and cool the onions.

4. Toast the bread cubes in a skillet with butter. Add one-half of the reserved onion pieces, chopped finely, and continue cooking until golden brown.

5. Toss the Gruyère cheese with the bread cubes and onion, orange zest, raisins, herbs, and salt and pepper, and sprinkle with armagnac. Mix well. This will not be a moist "stick-together" stuffing but the cheese will bind it as it melts and the crispy texture of the toasted bread will complement the melting onions.

6. Fill the onion cavities with the mixture and place in an oiled baking dish. Bake onions in their skins for forty-five minutes to one hour. (The longer they bake, the sweeter and softer the onion becomes.)

BROUTES DE CHOUX
Cabbage Shoots
Serves 4

These tender young shoots appear in the fall as the first cabbages harvested send off new shoots in the mild fall growing days. You can use any tender dark green cabbage-like plant—kale, beet greens, Swiss chard—just vary the cooking time to the texture of the green. One rainy fall day after a trip to the market at Casteljaloux, I piled the cooked greens on grilled toast, dressed them with oil, vinegar, salt, and pepper, and ate the little open-face sandwiches while the sausage was grilling in the fireplace.

1 bunch fresh tender cabbage shoots or other leafy greens
4 slices toasted country bread
1 clove garlic
2 tablespoons olive oil
2 teaspoons wine vinegar
salt and freshly ground pepper, to taste

1. In a pot of boiling salted water, cook the greens, whole or chopped in half, until tender. A pressure cooker can be used to reduce the cooking time; in this case, add just enough water to cover the greens.

2. Remove, drain, and chop finely by rolling the leaves up and slicing across the stem in narrow strips.

3. Pile the cooked greens on a piece of toasted bread that has been rubbed with a garlic clove. Sprinkle greens with oil, vinegar, salt, and pepper. Eat warm and be surprised!

This rustic dish goes well with the other savory flavors of country cooking—ham, sausages, boudin. For a dinner entrée, try putting the greens in a hot serving dish before dressing and serve with a slice of salty country ham that has been grilled and covered with shallots. Serve garlic-rubbed toast on the side.

COURGETTES AU BEURRE DE MENTHE DE MELINDA
Melinda's Zucchini with Mint Butter
Serves 4

Melinda, my French "little sister," taught me to rediscover the often overused zucchini (*courgette*). One evening when we were preparing a last-minute dinner on the *Julia Hoyt*, she offered to make the entrée. A market basket heaped with tender young squash caught her eye. I watched as she carefully cooked the thick slices until each was a perfect golden-brown circle. Melinda dipped one of the crispy rounds in mint butter, sprinkled a bit of sea salt on the edge, and handed it to me. It was so sweet! Somehow the simple magic of thought and care transformed this omnipresent vegetable into a special treat. *Merci, ma petite soeur.*

1 lb (500 g) young and tender fresh zucchini (courgettes), sliced in 1/2-inch (1 cm) rounds (Use only very fresh produce!)
1 tablespoon peanut oil
1/4 cup (2 oz/60 g) sweet butter
several fresh mint leaves, crushed and chopped finely
coarse sea salt, to taste
fresh white pepper, to taste

1. Place the zucchini rounds on a clean dishtowel and pat dry.
2. Pour the oil into the bottom of a large sauté pan and heat over medium heat. Lay the separate rounds side by side in one layer across the pan. Cook until golden brown then turn. Repeat until all the squash is cooked. Keep the first batch hot by placing on a cookie sheet in a warm oven.
3. While you cook the zucchini, prepare the mint butter. In a small mixing bowl, work the softened butter with a fork until it is creamy. Mix the mint leaves, salt, and pepper into the butter and let sit at room temperature.
4. When all the zucchini rounds are cooked, serve them on a platter and pass the bowl of butter around along with the salt cellar of coarse sea salt. Or arrange a little heap of zucchini on individual plates and garnish with a dollop of butter, a mint leaf, and a sprinkling of salt. Pass the pepper grinder and enjoy!

GRATIN DE POIREAUX
Leek Gratin
Serves 4

The sweet onion flavor of leeks, slow-cooked with cream and cheese, is a classic in country kitchens. As an entrée, leeks are a year-round substitute for the short-season asparagus, aillets (green garlic), and other delicacies.

6 large leeks
1 tablespoon sweet butter
1 cup (8 fl oz/250 ml) crème fraîche
1 cup (4 oz/120 g) Gruyère or Emmenthaler cheese
salt and freshly ground pepper, to taste
freshly ground nutmeg

1. Preheat the oven to 375 degrees F (190 C). Trim the roots and green tops off the leeks. (Save the greens for soup.) Slice the leeks lengthwise within 1 inch (3 cm) of the root end. Wash well under running water. Place them in a saucepan and cover with water. Add salt, cover, and bring to a rolling boil for fifteen minutes.

2. Drain the leeks well, pressing excess water out with a cloth or a wooden spoon. Cut the leeks in half.

3. Butter an oven-proof pan or casserole and place the leeks in one layer.

4. Spoon the crème fraîche over the leeks and sprinkle with cheese. Add salt and pepper and grate a dusting of fresh nutmeg over the surface. Bake for thirty minutes or until golden on top. Serve bubbling hot from the oven.

Note: The addition of a thin slice of ham wrapped around each leek piece before it is placed in the pan adds another delicious Gascon touch.

WILD LEEKS

One March morning, I saw from out of the salon windows across the canal two bereted older gentlemen walking and stooping, stopping and bending, then walking and stooping again. It drove me mad! What were they doing along the grassy towpath? What were they finding? I saw no basket for mushrooms, no bag for fallen walnuts. As casually as I could, I threw on a jacket and went for a walk.

"*Bonjour, messieurs.* What are you looking for? *Champignons?*"

"*Non, non...*" one replied. "*Des asperges de la pauvre...des poireaux sauvages.*"

Asparagus of the poor, wild leeks! They pulled from their pockets the thin-as-pencils green grassy shoots not unlike wild asparagus but with a tiny bulge of white at the bottom. They showed me how to spot them amongst the grasses. The leek leaves were flatter and broader than the others. They pointed down the canal and sent me off to hunt in fertile territory. I learned to use my finger as a little shovel to gently plow under the root and extract the delicate prize with a quiet "plop."

There have been many platters of early wild leeks since then, my first spring in the long village. Asparagus of the poor is the romantic name given the leek. But the leek, like its cousins the onion, garlic, shallot, and chive, is a gastronomic building block in the French countryside. And although none of my regional cookbooks bother to feature the leek in any recipes, I know that it's served in bistros and in homes, as a starter and in soups, in tourtes or gratins, served grilled and braised. I love the mild oniony flavor when it's set off by a cream sauce spiced with fresh nutmeg or bathed in a mustardy vinaigrette. At Michel Guérard's newest restaurant, La Ferme aux Grives, an elegant tribute to rustic cooking, I ate leeks that had been grilled over a wood fire and served with fine shavings of *jambon de Bayonne.*

Jambon Grillé aux Figues
Grilled Ham with Figs
Serves 4

The sweet melon and salty ham starter of summer is a classic combination enjoyed from July through September. This elegant fall version using ripe figs appears as the days chill down. This is a nice textural change between soup and main course. Pears, which are available into winter, may be substituted for figs.

8 paper-thin slices jambon de Bayonne, prosciutto, or Serrano ham
4 large ripe fresh figs, sliced
freshly ground pepper, to taste

    1. Grill the ham briefly under a hot oven broiler or over a barbecue grill until hot and starting to curl.
    2. Arrange the sliced figs in fans and place on plates.
    3. When the ham is done, arrange on the plates next to the figs.
    4. Crack a little fresh pepper over the whole and serve with a glass of sweet white wine.

Tourte aux Poireaux et Champignons
Leek and Mushroom Pie

A tourte is a savory crusty pie, usually no thicker than an inch with a thin, rich crust on the bottom and a thinner, richer crust on the top. This classic combination of leeks, mushrooms, and cream sandwiched between flaky bites of buttery pastry was taught to me by my "kitchen godmother," Vetou Pompèle, and is a *Julia Hoyt* favorite. Think of this tourte as a book of thin pages; layers of subtle flavors unfolding between covers of golden crust!

savory pastry crust (see following recipe)
1 lb (500 g) leeks
1/2 lb (250 g) mushrooms, brushed clean and with stems removed
1 egg
3/4 cup (6 fl oz/200 ml) crème fraîche

salt and freshly ground
   pepper
freshly ground nutmeg

1. Preheat the oven
to 425 degrees F (220 C).
2. Wash and trim
the leeks and keep just
the white parts. (Save
the greens to flavor a
soup.) Slice the leeks
very thin and wash
again in copious
amounts of water until
they are free of all grit.
3. Drain the leek slices

In the armagnac cellars

briefly and, while they are still wet, put them in a dry, heavy sauté pan over
medium heat. Stir gently as the leeks cook in their own water, about five minutes, until they are half-cooked.

4. Slice the mushroom caps very thin.

5. Place the pastry bottom in the tart pan and prick the bottom all over with
a fork. Beat the egg in a bowl and use some of it to brush the bottom pastry
before filling. This helps keep the juices from soaking into the crust.

6. Place the leeks in a layer across the pan. Top with a layer of mushrooms
and then spoon crème fraîche evenly over the filling. Salt and pepper generously and dust with nutmeg.

7. Place the thinner pastry layer on top and seal the edges with the bottom
layer by gently pinching the dough. Brush the remaining beaten egg over the
edges and surface of the tourte.

8. Bake about thirty minutes until golden brown and steaming hot. Serve hot
between courses or let cool to room temperature and serve with aperitifs.

PÂTE BRISÉE SALÉE
Savory Short Crust
Makes a 2-layer 10-inch (25 cm) tart crust

2 cups (10 oz/250 g) all-purpose flour
1/2 teaspoon salt
1/2 cup (4 oz/125 g) sweet butter
1/2 cup (4 fl oz/150 ml) water

1. Place the flour and salt in a bowl and add the butter, broken up into small bits.
2. Work the butter into the flour with your fingertips until crumbly and even in texture, or use a food processor or hand tool. Stir in water and mix quickly and lightly until the dough holds together. Do not overwork the dough. Pat into a ball and let rest while you are preparing the filling.
3. Divide the dough, rolling two thirds of the dough for the bottom crust and the remaining third thinner for the top crust. Work the dough gently and with sufficient flour to handle. The top crust should be very fine.

TOURTE AUX CHAMPIGNONS SAUVAGES
Wild Mushroom Pie
Makes one 10-inch (25 cm) pie

One October day, I returned to the *Julia Hoyt* to find two baskets of mushrooms sitting in the middle of the gangplank. One basket was filled to the brim with chanterelles, the other was full of black trompettes de la mort, also called "poor man's truffles." Underneath the baskets was a large picture book about mushrooms with the two pages devoted to my present marked with a little note... *"C'est très bon dans une omelette."* Who was my secret benefactor?

Odette, my shy gift-giving neighbor, returned the next day to retrieve her baskets and book. She explained that as a little girl during the war, she had known some American GIs who had supplied her family with extra rations and the now-famous chocolates and chewing gum. This was her way of paying back and welcoming us to the neighborhood.

I quickly discovered the mushrooms *are* good in omelets, great with parsley and cream on toast, and wonderful in little mushroom pot pies. I use small earthenware dishes to make these individual "wild pies" and often serve this at lunch with a salad of assorted wild greens. They are equally delicious as a starter to an autumn menu of game and woodsy fruits. The mushroom mix should combine textures and tastes. I add some dried morels or cèpes for flavor when I use domestic varieties.

savory pastry crust for one large or four
    small covered pies (see recipe, page 82)
2 lb (1 kilo) assorted mushrooms
1 tablespoon butter or duck fat
1 clove garlic, crushed
1 shallot, chopped
1 cup (8 fl oz/240 ml) red or white wine
1 tablespoon Dijon mustard
1 small bunch chives, chopped
1 handful parsley, chopped
1 egg

1. Preheat the oven to 425 degrees F (220 C).

2. Clean the mushrooms and chop in rough-sized pieces, leaving any small buttons whole. The larger the pieces, the more texture the pie will have.

3. Heat the fat in a heavy sauté pan over medium heat and add the garlic and shallot.

4. When the vegetables are wilted but before they start to brown, add the mushrooms. Cook, stirring gently with a wooden spoon, until the mushrooms start to give off their juices. Add the wine and mustard and cook for five minutes, stirring occasionally. (If the liquid starts to evaporate too much, put the cover on.)

5. Remove from heat and let cool slightly. Add the chives and parsley and stir.

6. Break egg into a mixing bowl and stir for an egg wash.

7. Roll out two-thirds of the pastry for the bottom of the tourte. Brush the pastry shell with the egg wash. Spoon the mushroom mixture into the pastry shell and cover with a pastry top. (I decorate the top of the pastry lid with a pastry cutout of a mushroom.)

8. Bake for thirty-five minutes or until pastry is golden brown. This rich, savory pie is delicious served with a glass of good red wine!

DUCK AND GOOSE FAT

Duck and goose fat are the distinctive cooking oils used in Southwest France. Rendered slowly from fowl fattened to produce foie gras, these pure poultry fats have half the cholesterol of butter and are typically used sparingly in these recipes. Ducks and geese have been fattened for their "oil" since the Egyptian pharaohs ruled; the force-fed fowl were the Jewish and Muslim kitchen alternative to the pork larder. Snowy white duck fat is delicate in flavor, while the richly flavored, butter yellow *beurre de foie gras* that is rendered from the fatted liver itself is prized for the character it adds to potatoes, soups, or as a simple spread on warm slabs of toasted country bread. Of course, you can substitute pure olive oil or other cooking oils in the recipes, but remember that you are substituting one flavor for another and compensate in the seasoning. When you buy your next jar or can of foie gras, remember to save the layer of fat from around the liver and use it to sauté a pan of crispy potatoes.

SALADE JULIA HOYT
Serves 4

Call it a Salade Gasconne or a Salade Landaise, this duck-topped salad is served in bistros, cafes, and restaurants across Southwest France. Greens from the valley

are topped with various duck meats and ham and pine nuts from the forests. I make it differently nearly every time depending on the stock in my "duck pantry": foie gras, *confit gésiers* (preserved gizzards), *cou farci* (neck sausage), *jambon de magret* (dried duck breast) or fresh *aiguillettes* (duck tenderloins). If I am rich with jars rimmed with golden yellow fat and little tins with handprinted labels, I use them all and call this lunch! If I want to introduce my guests to the complexities of the duck cuisine in Gascony, I parcel out the favored morsels, gésiers and foie gras, and use this to introduce a *menu de canard*, a duck dinner.

three lettuces: frisée (curly endive), red
    lettuce (lola rosso or oak leaf), and
    butter lettuce
1 handful pine nuts
8 oz (220 g) foie gras de canard
1 handful lardons (bacon cubes cut in
    1/4-inch (5 mm) pieces)
4 to 8 oz (100 to 220 g) confit gésiers
croutons
2 tablespoons wine vinegar
2 tablespoons salad oil
salt and freshly ground pepper, to taste

    1. Wash lettuce and dry. Arrange
the lettuce on large plates.
    2. Lightly toast the pine nuts in a
dry sauté pan over low heat. Be careful;
they burn easily. Set aside.
    3. Slice the foie gras and place on the salad greens.
    4. Put the lardons or bacon in the still-warm sauté pan and cook over medium heat until partly crispy. Slice the gésiers into thin slices and toss into the pan with the lardons. When the meat is hot, remove it with a slotted spoon, leaving any fat in the pan. Place the cooked meat on the salad. Add the croutons.
    5. Leaving the pan over the heat, stir in the vinegar and oil. Pour the hot dressing over the salad and sprinkle with salt and pepper. Serve this *salade composée* with a crusty baguette of bread.

FOIE GRAS AND THE FATTED DUCK

As the *Julia Hoyt* slowly cruises through the long village, the sight of a grassy field of grazing ducks greets us again and again. Here, in the open-air pastures, dozens of  mottled ducks, Mulard, Rouen, or Barbarie breeds, are fattened for family consumption. Two or three weeks before Christmas they will be brought into the barns and fed, by hand, a rich diet of cooked cracked corn. The fattened liver or foie gras is the prize for all this effort and it will be preserved in terrines or jars and kept to age in cool dark pantries. The tender leg and breast meat will be preserved as confit de canard, layered in glazed yellow pots and covered with snowy white fat. The flavorful fat rendered from underneath the skin is the basis for almost all of the cooking of Southwest France. Nothing goes to waste on a fattened duck.

In most Gascon households, foie gras is still a rare treat reserved for special occasions—weddings, baptisms, or fêtes—that demand the luxury of this silken-textured duck liver. Served simply with toasted bread and a sweet white wine, this special course takes the place of honor in a menu before the entrée, the first course. In the past, at a formal banquet, foie gras would be served in aspic or with truffles after the main course as a sort of savory dessert. In recent years, foie gras has become popular as a main course dish on luxurious restaurant menus.

Foie gras production has become a year-round farm business, as restaurants and gourmet shops all over Europe require a continuous supply to satiate growing appetites. Gascon farms are alive with choruses of hundreds of quackers as *artisanal conserviers* (cottage industry producers) prepare the fattening pens and their *laboratoire*-kitchens for the intensive two-week period of *gavage* (force-feeding). The resulting "surplus" of high-quality duck meat has led to the development of new dishes like grilled *magret du canard*, the breast of a fatted duck, and the commercialization of *confits de canard*, formerly popular only among farmers as a way of preserving the meat for future use.

For the very best foie gras, I search out the small producers who hand-feed their flocks and conserve the products with great care. I buy in small village markets and directly from the farms when I spot a handpainted sign that announces *"foie gras fermier."*

Like wine, foie gras is classified, labeled, and usually priced according to the contents. *Foie gras entier* is nothing more than the best pure foie gras in its natural form, the whole perfect lobe or part of a lobe, lightly seasoned and packed in a jar or can. The sterilization process "cooks" the foie gras in its packaging. *Foie gras de canard* is just the liver, too, but it is smaller pieces and therefore is less expensive. *Bloc de foie gras* is also just the liver but it is composed of small bits and imperfect-looking livers, processed into a paste and re-formed in the jars or tins. The next step down the foie gras ladder is *parfait de foie gras*, and then *pâté de foie gras*, which is foie gras mixed with other meats and fillers. Of course, the best way to savor the delicate results of the ancient art of gavage is to sample fresh foie gras cooked quickly and simply.

My mentor in all things relating to ducks is the generous Gascon chef Maria-Claude Gracia, who welcomes my visits to her fourteenth-century mill auberge, La Belle Gasconne, in her native village of Poudenas. Maria-Claude and her husband, Richard, prepare and serve terrine de foie gras from ducks raised under their supervision and prepared in their spotless restaurant kitchens. They devote whole winter weekends to teaching eager cooks the forgotten ways of confiture and preserving. I have learned from her the way to serve *foie gras frais* (fresh foie gras). Maria-Claude sautés and serves the pale firm livers with salad greens dressed with a vinaigrette. Fruit vinegar is used to deglaze the hot pan and mingle with the foie gras juices. I serve this on the *Julia Hoyt* when I introduce my guests to foie gras, to help explain the succulent difference between a pâté, a mix of meat or poultry with seasonings, fat, and sometimes fillers, and a piece of the whole liver, the foie gras entier.

SALADE DE FOIE GRAS CHAUD
Salad with Sautéed Fresh Foie Gras
Serves 4

1 fresh foie gras (Average weight of a foie gras is 1 to 1 1/2 lb.)

Vinaigrette
2/3 cup (5 fl oz/160 ml) peanut oil
1/4 cup (2 fl oz/60 ml) red wine vinegar

Salad
lettuce leaves (at least 3 kinds, mixed)
2/3 cup (5 fl oz/160 ml) fruit vinegar
(see recipe, following)

1. Devein the raw foie gras if necessary, and slice into 1/2-inch (15 mm) slices. Arrange on a plate and leave in the refrigerator until ready to cook.

2. Mix the vinaigrette. Lightly toss the rinsed and dry lettuces in the vinaigrette and place on plates.

3. Place the foie gras slices in a heavy-bottomed sauté pan over medium heat and lightly brown on both sides. This only takes a few minutes. The liver will be medium-rare, or *mi-cuit*.

4. Salt and pepper both sides of the liver. Then place the cooked pieces of foie gras to one side of the lettuce on the waiting plates. Do not blot the slices of liver; the juices from the foie gras will mingle with the vinegar to form a sauce.

5. There will be a certain amount of golden fat rendered from the liver. Each liver will yield a different quantity. Pour off all but a couple of tablespoons of the fat. The excess fat can be stored in a jar in the refrigerator.

6. Deglaze the pan by pouring in the reduced fruit vinegar and stirring over medium-high heat. Reduce briefly until the vinegar has started to thicken and become syrupy. Drizzle the vinegar over the foie gras. Place some of the fruit from the vinegar alongside the foie gras as garnish.

VINAIGRE DE FRUITS
Fruit Vinegar

Fruit vinegars can be made with whatever fruits are in season—strawberries, cherries, melon, prunes, peaches, grapes, pears. These concentrated sweet/acidic flavors are excellent for basting meats and poultry that are roasted or grilled. The whole fruit poached in the flavored vinegar is delicious as a garnish or added to various dishes. Glass jars of jewel-tone fruit steep in many-colored vinegars in the bistro-galley, adding a sharp spicy element to the pantry. Both pear and prune vinegar go especially well with foie gras.

2 cups (16 fl oz/500 ml) wine vinegar (Use red wine vinegar for prunes and dark
    fruits; white wine vinegar for peaches and light fruit.)
1/4 teaspoon freshly grated nutmeg
2 to 3 whole cloves
1 cinnamon stick
3 tablespoons sugar
salt and freshly ground pepper, to taste
1 lb (500 g) very ripe fruit (Use only the ripest, most fragrant fruit.)

    1. Combine all of the ingredients (except fruit) and one-half of the chosen fruit in a large, non-reactive saucepan. Using a fork, break up the fruit in the vinegar.

    2. Simmer over medium-low heat until the liquid reduces to a consistency of a light syrup, about fifteen to twenty minutes.

    3. Strain the fruit by pouring through cheesecloth, a coffee filter, or other fine mesh, and return the clear liquid to the saucepan. Poach the remaining fruit in the liquid, very briefly. Strawberries and soft fruit need only a few seconds, cherries and firm fruit a minute or two at the most.

    4. Place the poached fruit in a glass or pottery container and cover with its vinegar. Store in a cool dark place to use in salad dressings, or as a marinade for roasted meats and game. A tablespoon of this rich fruity vinegar over fresh fruit adds a distinctly Gascon touch to dessert.

Le Mas d'Agenais
and Lagruère

THE PAST IS always part of the present on this quiet waterway. Images of mule-drawn wooden *barques* are just around the corner as we glide past stone bridges scored by countless taut haul ropes on the approach to Le Mas d'Agenais, the midpoint of our journey. It's not how many kilometers we cover in a day that counts, it's how many centuries we've travelled.

Le Mas d'Agenais, like its Roman counterpart Meilhan, sits high on a bluff overlooking the Garonne and its canal. Flanked by a vast and rich forest, this naturally noble site once held sacred by the Celts and Druid priests is now valued by gastronomic pilgrims searching for cèpe, *girolle*, and trompette de la mort mushrooms. These earthy treasures punctuate the cuisine of the Garonne Valley, where mushrooms are sautéed, stewed, preserved, pickled, and dried. Like plucking escargots from wet leaves on a moonlit evening, mushroom hunting has its diversionary qualities, too. In the time before television, this was entertainment, exercise, and education as well as gastronomy.

The D6 road crosses the valley from route N113 and arrives at Le Mas d'Agenais by crossing both the river and the canal in one graceful series of Moorish arches. The striking village crest of three red hands signals our arrival. By canal, we arrive via écluse #44, Écluse de Le Mas, complete with tidy lockhouse, green shutters, singing canary, and rose garden in bloom. Mirrored in

The handprint shield of Le Mas

the port are the chaotic medieval houses that roost on the escarpment's edge, gardens spilling down the hillside, and a dozen or so boats that are tied to water and electricity. Crews climb past the old *lavoir* (washhouse) and along the Roman brick walls to reach the butcher, baker, hardware store, and the village church graced by its own Rembrandt treasure.

The long village has a special shape. It is stretched and narrow and has a definite hump in its center like the cartoon snake from St. Exupery's *Le Petit Prince* featured on the new 50 franc notes. If there are more stories and recipes from Lagruère than from any other place on the canal, it's because Lagruère, the midpoint of the long village, is the *Julia Hoyt's* second home on the canal. Older than the Roman sculpture of the "Venus of Mas d'Agenais" and the artifacts found in the surrounding fields, Lagruère has long been a feeding stop. *"Grue"* means crane and Lagruère is where the northern common cranes rest and feed on their annual migration to winter havens in Africa. Nature ruled this lazy horseshoe bend on the Garonne, flooding the great mother river and creating a supermarket of frogs and small fish for feeding birds. High overhead one November morning I heard their faraway call...over 120 cranes in a giant arrow shooting south across the valley.

The first time the *Julia Hoyt* stopped at Lagruère, the entire village was preparing for the first annual Fête du Canal, a rural celebration of music, dancing, food, and fun to inaugurate the newly built snack bar at the canal-side dock, the Halte Nautique. We slowly idled our way past a group of volunteers stringing colored lights for the fête. In my awkward best French, I called ashore as they stopped to watch our arrival, "Is it possible to moor here for the night?"

"*Oui, bien sûr*," came the response.

"Is it possible to get electricity?"

"*Oui, oui*," a young man nodded.

"And water, is that possible, too?"

"*Tout est possible à Lagruère!*" was the reply.

And so it was. Not only was everything possible at Lagruère, but it was done with great pride. The *Julia Hoyt* became a part of the Fête du Canal and we were invited to stay as long as we liked. It's been five years now! This farming community of 350 became the heartbeat of my long village as the *Julia Hoyt* was accepted into the tight community and we were adopted by what we've come to know as *le Famille*, the Pompèle family.

POULE AU POT CHEZ POMPÈLE

On my night off from the bistro-galley, I look forward to sharing the evening's gastronomic ritual with Patrick and friends as we tie up alongside the Halte Nautique at Lagruère and walk up the hill to the garden gate across from the World War I memorial. Through the gate and past the ever-present *potager* (kitchen garden) spilling tomatoes, peppers, zucchini, and salad greens over the path, the front door stands ajar and the fragrances of home cooking rouse our senses. "*Teh, des Américains arrivent.*" That's Claude, just ascending from the basement and his *cave* with a couple of bottles of homemade aperitif in hand. Every French house has its favored aperitif, pastis or muscat, rivesalte or kir gascon but at chez Pompèle it is the homemade vin de noix that Claude makes every year in the summer (see recipe, pages 24-25). Vetou is just pulling a golden *tourte aux champignons* from the oven in her crowded kitchen. Aperitifs are served around the kitchen table and I crane to peek into the giant pot that bubbles and steams

Reine de la Cuisine

in the open hearth in spring and autumn or out on the terrace over a gas ring in the sunny summer days.

The Pompèle's son Yannick and daughter-in-law Melinda arrive with baby Clotilde-Julia, who was half-named after a barge. The newest addition to the Pompèle family is passed around to admire and trade funny faces with. Her American godmother (me, of course) recounts the many courses served at her festive christening last month. Feast days and holidays are specially cherished by the family cooks who toil to leave a culinary souvenir, and tonight's dinner is typical of the special dinners prepared when family gathers to celebrate. Melinda has laid the enormous table in the dining room with handwoven white linen sheets, many wine glasses, and a vase of bright flowers picked from the backyard.

Vetou is *"Reine de la Cuisine"* (Queen of the Kitchen) here. Half Italian, half Breton, and all French, she has the wide wild eyes of the seagoing, storytelling people of Brittany. She always tells a story as she cooks dinner, and the story and dinner are somehow inseparable. She is what I imagine my wonderful Italian grandmother, Julia, was like when she was young. *"À table, tout le monde!"* Vetou sings, and Yannick whisks the flowers away just at the moment that Claude arrives with the golden soup tureen to plunk in the midst of our hungry group.

This is the beginning of a Gascon tradition that dates to the reign of King Henri IV, King of Navarre and later King of France. It was this fifteenth-century monarch who declared that the stuffed and poached chicken prepared for him was so good and healthful that "he wished all of his people to sup on this chicken-in-a-pot on Sundays." To this day, Poule au Pot or Poulet Henri IV is a traditional meal served in countless Gascon homes and dished up in two parts: first, the poaching broth as soup, then the chicken and its stuffing.

Vetou comes to the table wearing her apron like a military uniform, testimony to the long battles won in the kitchen. Straddling the long wooden bench, wooden spoon in hand and with the unfailing timing of a born actress, she tells us about *nostric Henri* (our Henry). History is ladled into every bowl as we spoon in the legends alongside the warming soup. "They say Henri was baptized with a garlic clove rubbed on his lips and a bottle of good Juraçon wine poured on his little royal head." Stories of his romantic exploits are kept alive throughout the Gascon countryside as soup bowls are passed and refilled with the rich golden broth that have bound story and recipe for over 400 years.

Claude then asks us if we would like to try another Gascon tradition. The tureen, refilled with hot broth, is passed around. Everyone takes another ladle of hot soup as Claude pours strong homemade red wine from a bottle with no label into each bowl. The warm, enriched broth is drunk from the bowl all in one go without the use of spoons. That is *"faire le chabrot."*

Soup bowls are cleared and glasses topped up in preparation for the arrival of the poule itself. The stewing chicken has been neatly stuffed both under the skin and in the cavity and has been cooking slowly in its own broth for the better part of the day. Sweet fat carrots, clove-studded onions, leeks, bay leaf, and more have perfumed the meat and broth. Now the bird is carved and served with its egg-rich stuffing. Two bowls of tomato-caper sauce are passed after the platters. Vetou places a jar of Claude's homemade cornichons on the table and the bilingual and fractured French conversation resumes.

In these Gascon homes a poule au pot is considered to be just the first part of a meal, an extended two-part first course. The French say *"Bon continuation!"*

THE MAIN COURSE

Like a modern story, a modern meal is told in chapters, in order. The introduction, the soup. A build-up, the entrée. A hump in the middle, the main course. A denouement, the dessert or cheese. A poached and stuffed chicken may be a culinary climax but it's nowhere near the end of the story. Rather, it serves as the festive beginning to a copious and abundant meal. An entrée, a bubbling casserole of creamy leeks, is served

next, before the main course, a roasted duckling with green olives and garlic, is brought to the table with a vast quantity of potatoes. Salad follows, and the baskets of bread are continually replenished. Two desserts, a *flan au Floc* and a tarte aux pommes precede the coffee and after-dinner digestives of eau-de-vie and armagnac. The wine-steeped pruneaux come last and cement the Franco-American relationship that has been built around the lively table.

The main course is the backbone of Gascon country cooking. Less noble cuts of meat, farm-raised poultry, and wild game are braised, stewed, roasted, and basted with the robust flavors I identify as "rustic." This *cuisine rustique* is passed from mother to daughter, from home cook to restaurateur. Slow cooking is the single common key to these recipes. Simple ingredients are scrupulously fresh and what all my mentors refer to as "*tout naturel.*"

In addition to the traditional recipes I learned in Claude and Vetou's home in Lagruère, I learned how to eat there. Time, attention, and laughter have been part of the lessons. Caught somewhere between farm and town, Vetou's exemplary French village kitchen reflects the intimate knowledge of careful cooking and caring hospitality. I learned to linger over our conversations, tell stories, and unwind at the table; everything tastes better.

CANARD AUX OLIVES
Duckling with Green Olives
Serves 4

In the farm kitchens that line my long village, chickens, geese, turkeys, guinea fowl, pigeons, rabbits, and ducks are roasted, stewed, simmered, braised, and preserved. A trip to the butcher for a roast beef or a piece of veal was a rare occurrence and limited to once or twice a year. Even today, when a family raises calves, as do my neighbors in Ste. Colombe, the meat is sold for income. Farm families eat what is at hand and usually found strutting around the farmyard. Now, throughout Southwest France, special crossbred ducks are also raised as a cash crop for both foie gras and confit.

This is a regional favorite prepared with a *canette*, a young female duckling that is a few months old and produces very tender meat. The green olives and garlic perfume the rich meat as they roast slowly in and around the duckling. Serve this with a summer crop of vegetables or a fresh green salad dressed with a walnut vinaigrette.

1 3 to 4 lb (1 1/2 to 2 kilo) duckling
1 tablespoon fresh thyme, chopped
sea salt and freshly ground pepper, to taste
1 whole head fresh garlic
1 cup (8 oz/125 g) green olives
thyme branches
1/4 cup (2 fl oz/60 ml) red wine vinegar
1 bottle dry white wine

1. Preheat the oven to 425 degrees F (220 C).

2. Rub the bird's inside cavity and the skin side completely with the thyme, salt, and pepper (or use some pepper and herbed sea salt, see recipe page 33). Place in a roasting pan.

3. Peel the garlic cloves and place with the green olives inside the cavity and around the bird. Place a few thyme branches inside the cavity. Sprinkle the wine vinegar over the bird. Place in the hot oven and cook for twenty minutes.

4. Turn heat down to 350 degrees F (180 C), pour two glasses of the wine into the pan, and continue cooking until done, approximately twenty-five minutes. (Cover with a tent of aluminum foil if the duckling starts to brown too much.)

5. When the duckling is done, remove it to a hot platter. Deglaze the pan with another glass of wine and scrape up the crispy bits, the garlic cloves, and olives to pour over the meat. Serve with a gratin of potatoes and zucchini crêpes.

MAGRET DU CANARD AUX QUATRE ÉPICES
Duck Breasts with Four Spices
Serves 4

In the same way that foie gras became a daily menu offering at fine restaurants, this finely textured dark meat, more like beef than poultry, became standard restaurant fare throughout Southwest France in the early 1980s. Traditionally prepared for confit, now the "duck-steak" is usually grilled with the skin and fat still on one side and served rare to medium-rare, sliced on the diagonal like a flank steak. Longer cooking produces tougher results, but those who enjoy well-done meat will approve of its flavor and texture. Shallots and vinegar are a classic treatment, as are green peppercorn sauces or sauces made from fruit vinegars flavored with melon or sour cherries. I like to use the classic combination of ancient spices known as quatre épices, once used to help preserve meats and complement their gaminess. The quatre épices mixture of pepper, cinnamon, nutmeg, cloves and/or ginger is widely used in Southwest France as the signature seasoning for civets, ragouts, pâtés, and terrines. I serve this with a crispy potato *galette* and celery root purée to complement the rich flavors of the meat and sauce.

1 pair duck breasts (1/2 breast per person)

Marinade
1 tablespoon juniper berries
1/2 teaspoon each ground cinnamon, nutmeg, and ginger
1/4 teaspoon each ground cloves and freshly ground black pepper
1/2 teaspoon salt

QUATRE ÉPICES

Quatre épices (four spices) is to dark meats what thyme and bay leaf are to white meats. Quatre épices is as often as not more than four spices and can be a milled mixture of nutmeg, cloves, pepper, cinnamon, ginger, or other pungent spices. Although available in France in jars like any other spice mixture, cooks have their own preferred proportions. The spices are best crushed freshly if possible and mixed to taste when preparing a dish. I always favor nutmeg and ginger. Pepper by itself plays a key in enlivening the flavors and fortifying the soups, sauces, and meats of Gascony, as there is little spiciness in this cuisine in the form of hot peppers or mustards. When a recipe calls for quatre épices, I'll mention the proportions that I like, but be your own tastemaker.

1 tablespoon Dijon mustard
1/4 cup (2 fl oz/60 ml) armagnac
1/4 cup (2 fl oz/60 ml) red wine vinegar
1/2 cup (4 fl oz/125 ml) red wine
2 tablespoons capers
1 tablespoon unsalted butter
2 tablespoons chopped chives

1. Pat the duck breast dry and score the fat side on the diagonal twice to form a diamond pattern.

2. Heat juniper berries in a dry, hot pan until shiny, then remove from heat. Be careful not to burn; this doesn't take long!

3. With a mortar and pestle, combine the four spices, pepper, juniper berries, and salt, and grind well. (Using fresh and whole spices produces a more pungent mixture than ground, packaged spices, so adjust your seasoning as needed.) Add mustard and armagnac and mix into a paste.

4. Rub spice paste into the meat and skin side of the duck breasts. Place meat in a pan or bowl and cover. Refrigerate until ready to cook; the meat may be refrigerated twenty-four hours or more. (If I am in my usual hurry, I prepare everything else needed for dinner while the duck breasts sit at room temperature and skip the marinating time.)

5. Remove duck breasts from refrigerator thirty minutes before cooking and bring to room temperature.

6. Heat a dry heavy skillet or sauté pan until quite hot, then place the duck breast skin-side down in the hot pan. After about five minutes, when the skin is well browned and the fat has started to melt, remove meat from the pan. Drain fat and give the pan a quick wipe with a paper towel. Replace the duck breast in the pan meat-side down and cook for five minutes more. Move meat to a warm plate in the oven while you prepare the sauce. (I usually cook the meat medium-rare. If someone prefers it more well-done, I slice off that portion and let it cook in the wine sauce as the sauce reduces.)

7. Deglaze the pan with vinegar, stirring up all the crispy bits. Add the wine and any leftover marinade and reduce the mixture by one-half by simmering briskly over medium heat.

8. While the sauce is reducing, slice the medium-rare breasts on the diagonal and fan each on warm plates or a warm platter.

9. Add the capers to the reduced sauce and remove from heat. Stir in the unsalted butter, adjust seasoning, and spoon the rich, spicy sauce over each breast. Sprinkle with chopped chives for garnish.

PINTADE À L'ARMAGNAC
Guinea Fowl Bathed in Armagnac
Serves 4

On the narrow road that runs between our homeport at Camont and Bellevue, the farm at the top, there is a red-and-white sign that reads "*Attention Troopeaux.*" This means "look out for flocks," and especially for the black-and-white-spotted, mango-shaped guinea fowl, which cluster and run right down the middle of the road in a bird-brain panic. I call them "designer chickens," as they sashay their fashionable polka-dotted feathers across the road to graze the field for grubs and leftover corn kernels. These free-running birds are farmhouse favorites as well as restaurant stars, with tender and flavorful meat more like wild game than domestic fowl. The lean, thin-skinned birds need a protective covering during cooking. I often use a slice or two of bacon across the breastbone as the bird roasts. The armagnac "bath" coats the inner cavity and under-skin of the bird and flavors it with the aromas of Gascony's own eau-de-vie.

1 whole guinea hen
1/2 cup (4 fl oz/120 ml) armagnac
salt and freshly ground pepper
fresh thyme
2 bay leaves
1 small head garlic, peeled
2 strips bacon
1 cup (8 fl oz/240 ml) wine

1. Preheat the oven to 425 degrees F (220 C).

2. Wash and drain the guinea hen.

3. Dry the inside cavity of the hen with a paper towel and gently loosen the skin between the breast meat and the legs. Using a pastry brush or just your fingers, rub armagnac on the meat under the skin, on top of the skin, and in the cavity. Give it a good bath! Next, rub salt and pepper on the skin and inside cavity and place a couple of thyme branches and the bay leaves under the skin against the breast meat.

4. Place the hen in a roasting pan and insert the garlic cloves inside the cavity. Lay a crisscross of two bacon strips over the breast meat and roast in the hot oven for twenty minutes until the bacon starts to crisp. Then turn the temperature down to 350 degrees F (180 C) and continue roasting until done, about twenty-five to thirty more minutes. Baste from time to time. If the bird starts to get too brown, cover with a loose tent of aluminum foil, being sure to let the steam escape.

5. When the *pintade* is done, remove from the oven and transfer to a warm platter. Deglaze the pan with the wine, stirring in all the crusty bits. Cut the hen in serving pieces and arrange the garlic cloves as garnish. Pour the wine glaze over the meat and serve with a Gratin de Pommes de Terre which you can cook in the oven at the same time (see recipe, pages 130-131).

ARMAGNAC

Parfum is the French word for fragrance and flavor, and in the culinary arts of Gascony there is no more important parfum than that of the locally produced brandy, armagnac. Armagnac inspires more poetic descriptions in regional cookbooks than any other single element and is lauded and cherished as the liquid embodiment of all things Gascon. The flavor of armagnac imparts a peerless rustic finesse to the regional dishes.

I use more armagnac in cooking on the Julia Hoyt than we ever drink. The vintage bottles that we search out and collect from hidden distilleries to savor after a fine meal are as unique and different from each other as bottles of 1923, 1940, and 1962 wines. But "the kitchen bottle" is the supermarket variety, which I use to "baste," "bathe," or lightly perfume farm-inspired cuisine. Armagnac scents crêpes, *civets*, and terrines, as well as stuffings, tarts, and roasts. Cognac, the more available cousin of armagnac from the Cognac district north of Bordeaux, can contribute the fire but not the flavor of a real Gascon armagnac. A particular continuous-flow still, as opposed to the Cognac region's double-pot still, and the use of local oak from the Armagnac region contribute to the differences between the rival areas.

In the days of the horse-drawn *alambic*, itinerant distillers traveled the Southwest to transform local farm wine made from Folle Blanche, Baco Blanc, and Ugni Blanc grapes into brandy. Poured into hand-built casks made from black oak trees found in the Armagnac area, the year's yield would be stored in ventilated *chais* (aboveground wine storage buildings) whose stone walls and tile roofs would turn black with an alcoholic fungus. Often aged for decades, a barrel might be sold to one of the noble armagnac houses in the town of Condom, where it would be blended and bottled or reserved as a special vintage. With the money earned, a farmer might finance a daughter's wedding, a new roof, or a first grandchild's christening. By now the once-clear brandy has colored the honey tone of oak, and the vanilla scent of the wood, so evident in the chai, marries with the fragrance of prune, hazelnut, violet, and cinnamon spices. An empty glass left unwashed overnight will still carry its heady and complex perfume the next day. This aromatic stamina is what flavors the region's favored dishes. Armagnac is available at most larger liquor stores and wine shops. Like cognac, armagnacs are graded and can be blended or bottled as a single vintage year. The price reflects the age of the brandy as well as the distilling house. The price of imported armagnac is worth the special flavor it gives to these recipes.

POULET FARCI À LA BISTRO-GALLEY
Poached Chicken and Stuffing à la Bistro-Galley
Serves 4—6

This is my interpretation of the classic cook-all-day stuffed stewing hen, poule au pot. If you have the time and can find the 2-year-old, 7 to 8 pound laying hens that Vetou Pompèle uses to prepare this classic dish, then use the recipe that she gave me for the traditional poule au pot (pages 105-107). If, like me, you are pressed for playing time in the kitchen, can only find a frying chicken that's barely learned to cluck, and yet love the flavors of root vegetables, herbs, and tender poultry, then try this modified version of the Gascon chicken-in-the-pot, with the stuffing on the side. I use an old-time Gascon soup tradition of making a stuffing when there was nothing to stuff and cooking it on top of a fava bean soup so the dish can serve as the evening meal.

1 oz (30 g) salt pork, cubed
3 shallots, peeled and halved
4 leeks, just the white part, trimmed and halved
4 carrots, cut in finger-sized pieces
4 stalks celery or 1 small celery root, peeled and cubed
1 4 lb (2 kilo) fresh chicken (reserve the giblets for the stuffing)
salt and freshly ground pepper, to taste
2 tablespoons herbes de Provence (thyme, savory, fennel, basil, and lavender) or use fresh herbs

1. Place salt pork in a 12-inch (30 cm) heavy-bottomed pan with a tight-fitting lid, over medium heat. Add shallots, leeks, carrots, and celery to the pan. Add 1 cup (8 fl oz/240 ml) of water and cover. Continue to cook as you prepare the chicken.

2. With a heavy, sharp knife or kitchen shears, cut down the chicken's backbone and open the bird flat. Rub the skin and the underside with salt, pepper, and herbs.

3. Lay the opened bird skin-side up on top of the cooking vegetables. There should be enough liquid to just reach the underside of the bird; add more water if necessary.

4. Cover and reduce heat to the lowest setting. Simmer gently for forty-five

SAUCE AUX CÂPRES
Tomato-Caper Sauce

3 to 4 shallots, minced
1 tablespoon duck fat or oil
2 tablespoons flour
1 small jar capers (approximately 4 fl oz/125 g)
2 tablespoons tomato paste
poule au pot broth (see recipe, pages 105-107) or water

1. Place shallots in a saucepan with the duck fat. Cook over medium heat until the shallots start to soften and become transparent. Sprinkle with flour and stir.

2. Add the jar of capers and their liquid to the pan.

3. Stir in the tomato paste with a little water and enough broth (about 2 cups (16 fl oz/500 ml) from the poule au pot to make it the consistency you like. You should have ample sauce to pass around two or three times as seconds are served. Cook for five to ten minutes at a simmer and serve with the chicken.

minutes to one hour. The chicken will poach on top of the vegetable and juices and will become very tender. While it cooks, prepare the "stuffing."

Stuffing
2 slices dry bread, crusts removed (the heavier the bread the better the stuffing)
1/4 cup (2 fl oz/60 ml) milk
1 clove garlic
1 shallot
several sprigs fresh parsley
chicken liver, heart, and gizzard
2 eggs
salt and freshly ground pepper, to taste

1. Soak the bread in a little milk. Squeeze the crumbs well until they are broken up and quite mushy.

2. Chop together: garlic, shallot, parsley, and chicken liver, gizzard, and heart.

3. In a large mixing bowl, beat eggs and add the bread, giblets, and herb mixture, and the salt and pepper. Mix well with a fork. (The consistency is of a thick omelet.)

4. Place a heavy sauté pan or nonstick omelet pan over medium heat. Spread the thick mixture in the pan and cook. Fold it in half, omelet-style as soon as it is firm enough to hold its shape. Cover, remove from heat and set aside.

5. When chicken is tender and thoroughly cooked, remove to a hot platter.

6. Place the "stuffing" in the pan on top of the vegetables and let steam for five to ten minutes until hot and cooked through. Carve the chicken into pieces and serve chicken and vegetables in a shallow bowl with a

Madame Vetou Pompèle and "chee-kun"

slice of the stuffing on top and some of the flavorful broth over it all. Or, serve a little of the broth first as a starter and make a tomato-caper sauce (page 104) to serve with the chicken and stuffing.

Vetou Pompèle's Classic "Poule au Pot"

The country kitchens of Gascony have long memories. Since Henri IV ruled Navarre (and later all of France), Gascons have been admonished to eat a chicken prepared in this manner for their Sunday dinner. That was 400 years ago. Poule au Pot is still a Sunday favorite.

Neither sophisticated nor refined, this classic country recipe has a profound influence on the regional cuisine. It is a dish rarely served in restaurants as the preparation time and logistics are more suited to home cooking, as is the archaic manner of eating the two-course dish. First the broth in which the hen has poached is served as the soup with pasta or garlic toasts added, then a little red wine is added to the bowls and another round of hot broth is passed. This rustic custom is called faire le chabrot, and the fortified soup is supped from bowls without the help of a spoon. Next, the tender chicken, stuffing, and vegetables are served with a piquant tomato-caper sauce or a mushroom cream sauce. All this is just the first course in an elaborately choreographed festive dinner either at home or in the village hall. Locally, the French call this *le bouilli*, the boiled course, and it is followed by an entrée, then le rôti, or roasted meat or fowl course, and double desserts, a tarte and a flan. No one leaves the table hungry.

1 6 to 8 lb stewing hen
salt and pepper

Stuffing
1 thick slice salt-cured, air-dried ham—jambon de Bayonne or prosciutto
3/4-inch (2 cm) slice ventreche, pancetta, or salt pork
chicken gizzard, heart, and liver
1 loaf stale French bread, crust removed
1 cup (8 fl oz/240 ml) milk
1/2 teaspoon nutmeg
freshly ground pepper, to taste
1 handful fresh parsley, chopped
1 onion, chopped finely
2 cloves garlic, chopped finely
2 shallots, chopped finely
some chicken fat from under the skin, minced very finely
4 eggs (The richer yolks of a farm fresh egg give the stuffing its characteristic gold-
    en color. A laying hen might still have several eggs in the cavity, and they
    should be used in the stuffing!)

bouquet garni (thyme, bay leaf, and parsley)
1 lb leeks (3 to 5)
1 lb (500 g) carrots
1 lb (500 g) onions
1 bunch celery
2 to 3 turnips
2 to 3 zucchinis
3 to 4 tomatoes
1 handful short vermicelli or other small pasta

1. Wash and dry the hen, then salt and pepper its cavity. Next, prepare the stuffing, as follows.

2. Chop the meats into small pieces. After soaking the bread in the milk and nutmeg, squeeze out the excess liquid and drain. Season the bread with pepper (salt isn't necessary because of the ham) and parsley. Add the onion, garlic, and shallots. Add the chopped meat and minced fat. Beat the eggs and add to the mixture. Work the stuffing well with your hands (like kneading dough) until all is carefully mixed.

3. Stuff the chicken's cavity. After loosening the skin from the breast meat, stuff under the skin as well.

4. Sew cavity openings together with a large needle and heavy thread. The hen should be carefully closed with no stuffing escaping. Take small stitches, pulling the skin over the openings carefully as you sew.

5. Put the stuffed and sewn hen in a very large stock pot half-filled with hot water. Add enough water to cover the bird. Add a generous bouquet garni. Bring to a boil, then simmer gently over medium heat for thirty minutes. Add the leeks and carrots.

6. Cook slowly for an hour, then add onions, celery, turnips, and zucchini (courgettes). When the bird is nearly done (2 1/2 to 3 hours total time), add a few tomatoes, to give the broth a rich golden color.

7. Pour some of the bouillon, enough for a soup, into a large pot and bring to a boil. Add a handful of pasta or tapioca. When the pasta is cooked, serve the soup as the first course.

8. After removing the chicken from the remaining broth, let drain, carve, and serve on a platter with some of the vegetables and with the stuffing cut into slices. Accompany the chicken with Sauce aux Câpres.

Lapin au Cresson
Rabbit with Watercress
Serves 4

Rabbit is one of the "house favorites" on the *Julia Hoyt*. Tender and lean white meat is prepared in a dozen different ways in Gascony. But this recipe came to me on a walk to the spring at Camont, our canal-side farmhouse, where Monsieur Dupuy has tended the watercress patch for nearly fifty years. On the way to fetch spring water for the table that summer morning, I imagined the farm-raised rabbits grazing in the watercress patch and *"Voilà! Lapin au Cresson!"* If entertaining, use only the "noble" pieces—saddle and hind legs. Reserve the rest for soup stock.

1 rabbit, cut into equal-sized pieces
salt and freshly ground pepper
2 tablespoons all-purpose flour
1 tablespoon duck fat or cooking oil
1 bottle dry white wine, less one glass
1 bouquet fresh sage, rosemary, and thyme branches
4 shallots, minced
1 onion, thinly sliced
2 bunches watercress, chopped
1 tablespoon Dijon mustard
4 tablespoons crème fraîche or heavy cream, optional

   1. After cutting rabbit into equal-sized pieces so they cook at the same pace, sprinkle with salt and pepper and dust with flour.

   2. Lightly oil a deep sauté pan that has a lid and place on medium heat. Place rabbit pieces in the hot pan and sauté until golden. Do not overcrowd. Cook in two batches if needed, moving cooked pieces to a platter.

   3. While the rabbit is browning (ten minutes or so) place wine in a saucepan on medium-high heat. When the wine starts to bubble briskly, flame the wine in the saucepan with a long match and let cook until flames go out, then remove from heat. Add fresh herbs and set aside to infuse. When all the rabbit pieces are browned, return them all to the pan; spread shallots and onion slices over the top and pour heated wine over all. Cover with a tight-fitting lid and reduce heat to

low. Let the rabbit, shallots, and onions cook in the wine at a very slow simmer.

4. When rabbit is tender and pulling away from the bone, move pieces to a warm platter and keep warm. Leaving the lid off the pan, turn heat up to medium-high and reduce liquid by half. Add chopped watercress and cook for three to five minutes more.

5. Remove from heat and purée the onion, wine, and watercress mixture, first removing any woody stems from the whole herbs.

6. Return to heat, stir in the mustard, and simmer until hot and bubbly. If using crème fraîche, remove from heat and add. Pour the peppery green sauce over the rabbit pieces. Garnish with whole fresh herbs and serve with a steamed bunch of sweet garden vegetables such as carrots, leeks, and celery.

HERBS AND SHALLOTS

When I ask a French friend, a village housewife, or the butcher in his one-shouldered apron how to prepare a pigeon, duckling, chicken, rabbit, or guinea hen, they all chant the same simple words like an ancient, magic incantation, *"Thym, laurier, échalotes, et ail."* Thyme, bay leaf, shallots, and garlic are repeated over and over like a children's rhyme learned in mother's kitchen. These are the herbs common to most of the savory dishes prepared here in the long village.

Underneath the diverse facade of regional Gascon cooking there lies a characteristic scent of the garden in the form of these close-at-hand herbs and shoots. Thyme grows wild on the rocky hillsides; bay bushes sprout in every garden. Garlic is used like a seasoning, just one or two cloves, crushed and added to the dish. Except for the famous garlic-infused tourin served on wedding nights to fortify the newlyweds with pepper and vinegar, garlic takes a backseat to the ever-present shallot.

Here in the southwest of France, the unrestrained hand tends to reach for the basket of shallots first. Raw or cooked, they are used with abandon. Shallots are used whole or sliced, chopped and wilted with vinegar, wine, or oil. The little gray shallot, small and tight like a papery thimble, is used mostly in cooking. The *"cuisse de poulet"* (chicken's leg) shallot, or salad shallot, is used for vinaigrettes and raw preparations.

Old-fashioned herbs like verveine (lemon verbena) and hyssop are used often, too. I remember one cook's words, that one should always cook rabbit with the herbs it would eat in the wild. *"Thym, laurier, échalotes, et ail..."*

LAPIN AUX PRUNEAUX D'AGEN
Rabbit Cooked with Prunes of Agen
Serves 4

I remember my first Easter in Gascony and the first stay at the port in Agen with the *Julia Hoyt*. I was preparing to offer a special Sunday dinner meal for my bargemates, a sort of culinary joke—an Easter rabbit dinner. The joke was on me as well, since I had never prepared rabbit before. I walked from the old port to the *marché couvert* (the covered market) and screwed up my courage to buy a fresh rabbit from the poultry stall. There among the chickens, turkeys, guinea hens, and quail were whole rabbits, half rabbits, and rabbit pieces already skinned, cleaned, and ready to cook. But how? I put my purchase in my basket and looked around for a wise soul. There, behind a counter heaped with carrots, celery, parsley, lettuces, and other vegetables, was someone's kindly grandmother, sorting through the wooden boxes of mushrooms.

"*Excusez-moi, Madame...*" I fished in my basket, hauled up the rabbit by the legs and asked in my very limited French, "How would you prepare this for dinner?" Without so much as a smile at my very foreign accent, she flew around the counter and started to list the ingredients as she popped them one at a time into a paper bag.

"Two small onions, a handful of shallots, a few carrots..." Plop, plop, plop, into the bag. A small bunch of thyme, two branches of a celery stalk, and some parsley. A small sack of prunes from the wooden drying rack were placed in my basket. Then, grabbing my hand, she led me across the market floor to the wine merchant and requested from him a half-bottle of modest white wine. When he placed a small square plastic bottle the size of a soft drink on the counter and said "*Deux francs et soixante-quinze centimes*" (the equivalent of 50 cents or so), I began to protest that I could certainly afford a full bottle (and a better one at that!). Madame the Greengrocer looked me square in the eye and said, "It's for the rabbit, dear, not the cook." I bought both bottles (one for the crew, one for the rabbit) and with my recipe in the bag, I walked quickly back to the boat before I could forget the sequence of ingredients. The dinner was a success and this classic dish from the prune-growing region of the Agenais has since become a standard on the *Julia Hoyt*.

1 rabbit (a large stewing rabbit rather than a fryer, if you have a choice)
salt and freshly ground pepper
2 oz (60 g) bacon, diced
2 onions, cut in quarters, or a dozen small pearl onions, peeled
2 shallots, halved
2 tablespoons duck fat or oil
2 tablespoons flour
4 carrots, cut in chunks
2 branches celery, cut in chunks
2 to 3 sprigs fresh thyme
1 tablespoon chopped fresh
    parsley
18 prunes, pitted
1 bottle red wine minus 1 glass

1. Joint the rabbit into pieces and season with salt and pepper.

2. In a large stewing pan with a lid, place the bacon and cook over medium-high heat. Toss in the onions and shallots and cook until they start to brown. Remove from pan and set aside.

3. Place the fat or oil in the hot pan and add the rabbit pieces. Sprinkle with the flour and brown on all sides. Add the carrots and celery and return the onions and shallots to the pan. Place the thyme, parsley, and half of the prunes in the pan. Pour the wine over the rabbit and make sure it is covered by the liquid, adding some water if needed.

4. Cover and cook over very low heat for forty-five to sixty minutes. Never let the mixture boil.

5. When the rabbit is very tender and starting to fall off of the bone, remove to a hot platter and hold in a warm oven. Add the remaining prunes to the sauce and with the lid off, reduce the liquid by one-third by simmering briskly. Serve the rich, dark sauce over the rabbit with the vegetables and prunes, alongside a generous helping of *patates etouffées* (see recipe, page 138).

RÔTI DE PORC AUX PRUNEAUX ET ÉCHALOTES
Roast Pork Stuffed with Prunes and Shallots
Serves 4—6

The country larders in Gascony are filled with glass jars of preserved, succulent, tender pork, salted hams hanging from the beams, spiced sausages, and pâtés ready to spread on crusty baguettes. In the chilly but sunny days of winter, whole days are set aside for the butchering of the pigs. Entire families, friends, and neighbors help out in the time-consuming preparation of the dry sausages, boudin noir, and various pâtés. I'm lucky enough to buy home-produced hams and sausages from my neighbors and various artisanal butchers like in the old days. Fresh pork of a very high standard is available, as well. One of my favorite recipes combines prunes d'Agen, armagnac, and fresh shallots stuffed in a tender pork loin. The flavors meld together as the pork roasts, and the resulting caramelized juices that run in the pan are poured over the sliced meat.

Bon appétit!

24 large soft pitted prunes
2 cups (16 fl oz/480 ml) red wine
1/4 cup (2 fl oz/60 ml) armagnac
2 1/2 lb (1 kilo plus) pork loin
3 shallots, minced
salt and freshly ground pepper, to taste
2 carrots, chopped finely
1 celery stalk, chopped finely
1 small onion, chopped finely
1 tablespoon olive oil
1/2 cup (4 fl oz/125 ml) red wine vinegar
1 tablespoon butter

1. Chop 6 prunes into small pieces and place in a small bowl with the rest of the whole prunes. Add the red wine and armagnac. Soak for thirty minutes to overnight.
2. Preheat oven to 350 degrees F (180 C).
3. Slit the pork loin lengthwise. Remove the whole prunes from the wine

and together with the minced shallots, stuff the pork loin generously. Season with salt and pepper and wrap and tie the roast with kitchen twine.

4. In a roasting pan on top of the stove, sauté the diced vegetables with the olive oil, stirring until golden brown and well caramelized. Remove the vegetables and set aside.

5. Deglaze the pan with vinegar, pour off the liquid, and set aside for basting.

6. Place the stuffed pork roast in the pan and cook forty-five minutes per pound, basting often. (Use a meat thermometer to test the doneness.)

7. When done, remove roast from oven, place on a warm platter, and cover with aluminum foil. The roast will continue to cook and the meat will relax and be more tender.

To make a sauce, after removing meat from the pan, drain fat, and place the pan on top of the stove. Add reserved vinegar and deglaze the pan again with wine and prune pieces. Stir the crusty bits from the bottom and boil gently to reduce the liquid to 3/4 cup (6 fl oz/180 ml). Whisk in the butter and reserved vegetables. Serve sauce with the carved roast.

PAUPIETTES DE VEAU
Stuffed Veal Bundles
Serves 4

In France, butchers have a respected place in the kitchen. More than just chopping pieces of meat, they coax, season, and teach. French home cooks have a vast array of ready-to-cook meals available that their local butchers have prepared. Among the platters of veal chops, scallops, and shanks there are little bundles tied with string and ready to cook in a mushroom sauce. Poetically called *"alouettes sans têtes,"* these "larks without heads" are tender, tasty packages of veal scallops and sausage that are easy to make at home once you get the hang of wrapping and tying. Although I am always eager to try new stuffings and other sauces, this tastes so good as is that I make veal *paupiettes* the same way each time. A rare occurrence in the bistro-galley! The bundles may appear small, but two per person is plenty as they are richly filled and sauced.

LES PRUNEAUX D'AGEN

The plums of Agen are the sweet souvenirs of forgotten crusaders of the thirteenth century who returned to France from Syria with the new fruit. They called it the "plum date." The fruit was presented to monks at the abbey in Clairac, and it was they who were among the first to graft the new variety to wild plum trees and transform the ripe fruit into long-conserving pruneaux, or prunes.

The passionate cultivation of grafted trees is followed throughout the year as closely and carefully as the grape production for wine. Clouds of white plum blossoms frost the orchards in spring. Hailstone storms and spring frosts threaten the early buds, and orchard owners fret at every weather report. By midsummer the dark green canopy of leaves is burdened by hundreds of purple plums, and the weight of the heavy fruit visibly pulls the branches closer to the earth. As harvest in August and September approaches, the ripening fruit sports a pale blue blush, giving the illusion that the whole orchard is covered with a violet netting.

Once gathered by hand in the apron skirts of quaintly coifed girls of the Agenais, the harvested plums are now machine-gathered and sent by tractors to waiting ovens. Washed, sorted, and graded, the plums are placed on trays in single layers and put into enormous gas ovens to cook for twenty-four hours. The lost moisture wrinkles the plums, but the slow cooking also transforms the sweet fruit flesh into a dark and sugary jam. Each plum, now a prune, is like a concentrated, self-contained package of flavor and natural sugar. The prunes are then racked, bagged, and rehydrated before packing. And all of this is done without chemicals or preservatives. From this point, prune delicacies are made—prunes steeped in wine or armagnac and syrup, or pitted prunes filled with marzipan or other flavored fillings; wrapped, boxed, and ribboned, they are a special gift from the Agen area.

In Gascon homes, prunes soaking in eau-de-vie wait in stoneware jars to be served to visiting guests just as we would offer a cup of coffee. In the kitchen the flavors they add to a meal are memorable—Lapin aux Pruneaux d'Agen, Roast Pork Stuffed with Prunes and Shallots, Prune and Merguez Sausage Brochettes, tiny quail stuffed with just one plump armagnac-steeped prune.

8 veal scallops, cut thin (or pound as needed)
salt and freshly ground pepper, to taste
1 lb (500 g) lean pork sausage
1 tablespoon oil
1 onion, chopped
2 shallots, chopped
2 tablespoons flour
2 tablespoons tomato paste
1 bottle sweet white wine
bouquet garni (thyme, bay leaf, parsley, and sage)
1 lb (500 g) mushrooms, sliced
1 teaspoon orange zest

1. Flatten the veal scallops with the flat of a large knife. Salt and pepper generously.

2. Place a spoonful of sausage on each scallop one-third of the way down the scallop. Roll the scallop around the sausage, tucking the meat around the stuffing until well rolled. Taking about two feet of string, place the bundle in the middle of the string, and tie; turn one-quarter turn and tie again; turn again and tie again. When you have a neatly tied packet of veal and stuffing, clip off any excess string and set aside.

3. Place veal parcels in a single layer in a hot, deep sauté pan with oil. Brown on all sides and remove from the pan.

4. Sauté the chopped onion and shallots in the oil left in the pan. Stir until they start to color, then add the flour and the tomato paste. Continue to cook and stir until the mixture starts to color then add nearly the whole bottle of wine (remember, it's okay to reserve a glass for the chef!).

5. Place the veal paupiettes and bouquet garni in the sauce, cover, and simmer slowly for forty-five to sixty minutes.

6. Add the sliced mushrooms and orange zest to the sauce and cook uncovered for another fifteen minutes. Serve with rice or pasta.

DAUBE DE BOEUF GASCONNE
Braised Beef in the Gascon Style
Serves 4—6

The Blondes of Aquitaine are neither a female rock group from Bordeaux nor the latest haircoloring product to be bottled and sold in France. Picture instead the elegant slow gait of nearly one ton of honey-colored cow crossing a green pasture. These highly prized beef cattle, les Blondes d'Aquitaine, are to Southwest France what Charollais are to Burgundy in the north and Black Angus to our American West. Muscular and lean, they produce the top-quality beef that sells in the chic markets of Paris and Lyons, while the local farmers who raise them eat duck and chicken. It is not uncommon for a farmer to sell a calf or cow to a butcher and then receive a cut of the prized veal or beef in return. While the Parisians and other city folk enjoy choice cuts prepared as *bifteck à la Bordelaise* with shallots and vinegar and *côtes de boeuf* grilled over restaurant stoves, the inhabitants of my long village turn the less expensive cuts of beef, the shanks and cheeks, into gastronomic works of art.

On a visit to *ferme* Bellevue, a three-generation-run family farm, Mesdames Yvette and Brigitte Sabadini, mother and *belle-fille* (daughter-in-law), shared with me their two different versions of a *daube de boeuf*. While we sat underneath the umbrella-like horse chestnut tree that had been thoughtfully planted by Yvette's grandmother and drank citron pressé (lemonade), two neighbor ladies arrived to buy fresh eggs. *Voilà*, two more recipes for the classic braised beef! Everyone has a variation; in the fall, Brigitte adds quinces to the beef as it simmers to thicken and sweeten the sauce; her neighbor uses the gelatinous cuts—the cheek, shank, and tail bones. Vetou Pompèle (my final authority in all things culinary) lines the bottom of the pot with pieces of pork rind and adds a couple of squares of dark chocolate at the end, as do many local cooks. Although essentially a winter dish, I have prepared a delicious daube midsummer using red currants to enrich the sauce. The only thing that all the cooks I spoke with agreed on was the length of cooking time: a minimum of three days! Try as I might to reduce the lead time, I bow to the wise ladies of the Gascon kitchens.

The trick isn't in the actual length of cooking time, but rather in the time *between* cookings. A daube cooked three hours in a row will not be as tender as one cooked for one hour a day on three consecutive days; there is "magic" in the resting process that allows the flavors to marry and the beef to tenderize. Typically, the beef is marinated the first day, cooked the second day for about an hour on a slow fire, and recooked a third day for another hour or more. A fourth day continues the process until the beef can be eaten with a spoon!

Cuts of beef that retain their shape and texture are best. If you don't favor the lesser cuts like shank, you can use a chuck shoulder roast or bottom round. They are preferable to midsection cuts that fall apart and lose too much flavor to the sauce. The wine selected for the marinade and sauce should be a full-bodied "rustic" wine that will impart to the final dish fruit flavors as well as tannins.

Although often cooked in a slow oven or on the back of a wood-burning stove, a daube can also be cooked on a stovetop. On the *Julia Hoyt*, I rarely use the oven except on chilly days when we benefit from the extra heat that it puts out. To cook slowly on the stovetop, use a "diffuser," a grill that sits between the pot and the flame and helps adjust the cooking heat to a very even and low temperature. My ever-practical brother, Jeff, reminds me that a slow-cooking electric crock-pot, probably gathering dust in some hidden corner of many kitchen cupboards, is perfect for making a daube.

Once I overcame the mental obstacle of the lead time, I learned to make this tasty classical beef recipe as an easy dinner for those days when wine tasting or touring the countryside kept me from the galley all day. I marinate the beef in the wine the day that I buy it and cook the daube the next day for the first time very slowly for two hours as we travel down the canal. Don't let it boil! On the next day, I just set it on a low flame for the final cooking after we return from an afternoon's outing. There's little more to do by then and once aperitifs are finished and vegetables are arranged, it becomes another bistro-galley last-minute meal. I've added the cornmeal dumplings as my truc américain and as a culinary tribute to the fine corn flour used in Southwest France.

1 bottle full-bodied red wine
1 bouquet garni (thyme, bay leaf, and parsley)
3 to 4 lb (1.5 to 2 kilos) trimmed boneless braising beef (shank, chuck shoulder, top round, or bottom round), cut in large cubes
salt and freshly ground pepper, to taste
2 tablespoons quatre épices (four spice mixture, see page 98)
2 tablespoons duck fat or olive oil
1 thick slice ventreche (salted, air-dried ham) or pancetta, cut in strips
several pieces uncooked pork rind if available, enough to cover the bottom of your casserole
2 to 4 whole cloves
2 onions, quartered
4 carrots, sliced
4 to 6 cloves garlic, crushed
4 shallots, halved
3/4 cup (6 fl oz/180 ml) armagnac
4 squares bittersweet, dark chocolate

1. Marinate beef in the wine with the bouquet garni overnight. The next day, remove the meat, reserving the wine. Pat the quatre épices into the meat cubes.

2. In a heavy-bottomed lidded pan, heat the fat, add the beef, and brown on all sides. Salt and pepper the beef generously and let cook a little while.

3. Add the ventreche and brown it with the beef. If pork rind is available, remove the meat and line the bottom of the pan with the pork rind, fat-side down, then layer the meat over this "lining." This not only flavors the daube but prevents the meat from sticking to the pan during its long cooking.

4. Stick the cloves into the onion quarters and add to the beef along with the carrots, garlic cloves, and shallots.

5. Heat the armagnac in a saucepan. When warm, flambé carefully and pour over the beef and vegetables. Continue to simmer over a slow heat.

6. Heat the reserved wine in the same saucepan that you heated the armagnac in, bring to a boil, and flambé. When the flames go out, pour over the beef and cover. Continue cooking over low heat. Use a diffuser if possible or place the pot in the oven at 250 degrees F (125 C). Cook for two hours.

7. Remove from heat and let cool, then place in the refrigerator overnight.

8. The next day degrease and cook again on low heat for sixty to ninety minutes. Correct the seasoning as needed. In the last thirty minutes, add 4 squares of bittersweet chocolate to the daube and stir until it's melted.

9. While the meat cooks, make the corn flour dumpling dough (see below). Cook the dumplings by placing heaping tablespoons of dough on top of the simmering daube, leaving ample room between them. Cover and cook for ten to fifteen minutes, until dumplings are firm and dry.

10. Serve the daube with the vegetables and dumplings as garnish and surrounded by the rich wine sauce. A good bottle of red wine, a vinegary green salad, and a crusty sugar tart are all that is needed for a deeply satisfying and robust Gascon meal.

CORNMEAL DUMPLINGS

3/4 cup (4 oz/125 g) finely ground yellow cornmeal (I regrind commercial corn-
    meal to a powdery texture in my coffee mill)
3/4 cup (4 oz/125 g) all-purpose flour
1 teaspoon baking powder
1/2 teaspoon salt
2 eggs
1/2 cup (4 fl oz/125 ml) milk
1 tablespoon melted butter

1. Combine the dry ingredients in a large mixing bowl. Beat the eggs and milk in a separate bowl and add the dry ingredients to it all at once. Stir briskly, then stir in the melted butter.

2. Drop from a spoon onto daube and cook as directed.

SAUMON SAUVAGE AU BEURRE D'ORANGE
Wild Salmon with Orange-Butter Sauce
Serves 2—4

This recipe is from my favorite restaurant in all of Southwest France, à La Belle
Gasconne, in the little village of Poudenas on the banks of the river Gelise. Here,
Marie-Claude Gracia reigns in the kitchen as her gracious husband, Richard Gracia,
welcomes us to sit in the fourteenth-century mill that they have so lovingly restored.
Although foie gras and duck is the traditional backbone of Marie-Claude's *"cuisine de
passion,"* her wild salmon with orange-butter sauce is one of my favorites. No festive
meal in Gascony is without a fancy fish course between the entrée and the meat
course, although this stands on its own here as a delicious main course or *plat principal.*

2 pieces fresh salmon filet
salt and white pepper
1 tablespoon extra virgin olive oil

Orange-Butter Sauce
1 orange (blood orange if available)
1/2 lemon
1/4 cup (2 oz/60 g) unsalted butter, room temperature
salt and white pepper, to taste
1 tablespoon chopped fresh parsley
1 tablespoon chopped fresh tarragon

   1. Salt and pepper both sides of the filets. Place a little oil in a heavy sauté pan
and put the salmon in the cold pan. Begin cooking over a slow fire. When the
salmon is lightly colored on one side, turn, cover, and finish cooking as it steams
in its own juices.

   2. Squeeze juice from the orange and lemon. While the fish continues cooking, put the butter and the juices in a small saucepan. Slowly soften over low
heat while beating with a fork until the liquid reaches the consistency of heavy
cream. Add salt and pepper and the chopped herbs at the last minute. Remove
from heat. (The butter should be hot but not boiling.)

   3. Place the cooked salmon on hot plates (it will be cooked thoroughly yet
still soft) and dress with the orange-butter sauce.

TRUITE FARCIE À LA POÊLE
Pan-Grilled Stuffed Trout
Serves 4

As we moor in the port before the last lock on our long village, l'Écluse de l'Auvignon, the glowing summer twilight is mirrored in the fish ponds at Bruch. Herons fly over the canal and frogs chant through the night as we put the grill out on the towpath and prepare a barbecue dinner. Summer nights are long in this part of Europe. The July sun doesn't set until 10:30 p.m.! We drink a chilled bottle of the local dry rosé wine as the coals begin to glow and the hilltop villages of Clermont-Dessous and Bazens light up the ridge of the Garonne Valley.

Truite truck

These foot-long, tender, pink-fleshed sea trout are members of the salmon family and are easy to bone before stuffing and serving. I like the twist on the classic trout and almond combination, and either grill these outside or, as in this version of the recipe, in a pan in the bistro-galley.

4 whole small trout (about 10 oz/300 g each), cleaned and boned
salt and freshly ground pepper, to taste
1 large handful fresh parsley, chopped
1 cup (6 oz/180 g) ground almonds
1 cup (2 oz/50 g) fresh bread crumbs
1 egg
1 tablespoon chopped fresh tarragon
2 tablespoons butter
1 cup (8 fl oz/240 ml) white wine

1. Salt and pepper the cavity and skin of the trout.

2. Mix the parsley, almonds, and bread crumbs together with the egg, tarragon, and more salt and pepper. Add a little of the wine if needed, to moisten.

3. Stuff the cavity of the trout and close the opening with a pre-soaked bamboo skewer or several toothpicks.

4. Place one-half of the butter in a heavy pan and melt. Add the trout just as the butter melts and cook over a medium-low heat until the trout is done on one side and the skin is golden brown. Turn the trout over carefully and cover, lowering the heat. Cook slowly about ten to fifteen minutes, until done. The stuffing should be hot and firm. Transfer the trout to hot plates.

5. Deglaze the pan with the white wine and whisk in the remaining butter. Pour this sauce over the stuffed trout. Serve with a purée of vegetables, and couscous or broiled tomatoes.

POULE VERTE: UN CHOU FARCI
Green Chicken: A Stuffed Cabbage
Serves 4—6

Gascon cooks are as imaginative as they are practical. Choosing a dark green ruffled cabbage at the morning market, they transform it into a delicious dish by midday and dub it a "green chicken." Taking the place of a stuffed poached chicken, the poule verte can serve as the soup and entrée for a grand rustic dinner or as a meal in itself. The cabbage is sliced into wedges, revealing the layers of stuffing sandwiched in between the leaves. I serve this with the same piquant tomato-caper sauce that accompanies a poule au pot (see recipe, pages 105-107).

1 medium savoy cabbage

Stuffing
1 cup (8 oz/250 g) chopped vegetables—onions, celery, fennel, and shallots
2 tablespoons melted butter or vegetable oil
1/2 cup (4 fl oz/125 ml) white wine
2 tablespoons chopped fresh mixed herbs (thyme, sage, and rosemary)
2 cups (4 oz/100 g) bread or cornbread

1/2 cup (4 oz/125 g) fresh pork sausage
1 egg

Broth
3 carrots, cut in large pieces
2 leeks, trimmed and cut in large pieces
1 onion, quartered
bouquet garni (thyme, bay leaf, and parsley)

1. Bring water to boil in large pot. Trim the cabbage of loose leaves and cut an "X" in bottom of core. Parboil the cabbage in boiling water for ten minutes.

2. In the meantime, sweat chopped vegetables in oil or butter until barely soft. Add wine and herbs, and cook for three to five minutes until soft. Pour vegetable mixture over bread crumbs and mix well. Add sausage meat and beaten egg to the bread crumbs and mix with your hands until you can form into a ball.

3. Remove the cabbage from water and drain.

4. Add the carrots, leeks, onion, and bouquet garni to a pot of boiling water. Simmer over a medium-high heat.

5. After cabbage has cooled, gently pry back the outer leaves until a small core of cabbage the size of the stuffing ball is revealed. With a small knife or by twisting the core, remove the cabbage heart, leaving the outer shell intact. Place stuffing ball inside in place of the cabbage core and refold the outer leaves carefully. Tie the outside leaves in place by wrapping in a cheesecloth square or tying with kitchen string. (Another stuffing method is to peel back the leaves and, starting as close to the heart as you can get, layer in spoonfuls of stuffing between leaves. Continue to do so until all the stuffing is used and the cabbage is tightly packed. Tie with the string to hold the stuffed cabbage together.)

6. Carefully submerge the "green chicken" in the poaching broth with the vegetables and simmer gently for twenty to thirty minutes. To serve, remove the tied cabbage and cut the string off. Let cool slightly while you prepare the bowls, then slice or quarter the cabbage and place a wedge in each bowl. Ladle soup broth and other vegetables over and serve with tomato-caper sauce drizzled over the top.

DAMAZAN, VIANNE, AND BUZET

Les Bastides

MORNINGS on the *Julia Hoyt* are peaceful. The first crew to rise quietly embrace a good cup of coffee and head out to the deck for a birdsong awakening. The tall plane trees offer a canopy of shelter to many types of birds, birds that signal the changing seasons as definitively as the tree's plate-sized leaves change from green to gold. There are over 45,000 plane trees growing along the canal, as well as poplars, chestnuts, oaks, cherry trees, walnut trees, and cypress. We slowly get under weigh with a great push of the bargepole off the roots that extend into the canal from these many trees. The next several hours are spent "keeping it between the trees" as we cruise the verdant tunnel between Lagruère and Damazan.

It was in the summer of tomatoes, the hot July of 1989, that we discovered Damazan and its maze of narrow streets squared off at right angles, all leading to or from the perfectly plotted town center. A gray stone church stands on the corner of the square. Two butchers, a hardware store, and an antique shop operate from beneath graceful stone arcades. The brush-lettered signs of the shoe store, bicycle shop, and *tabac* are faded echoes of the past, but four boulangeries and *pâtisseries* still perfume the morning with yeast and sugary scents. Although modern commerce has evaporated from

Monsieur Ryckman

Damazan in this century, on Thursday mornings the little covered square relives its history with a small market as it has for seven centuries.

Damazan is a *"bastide,"* one of the fortified planned towns, walled and built by the French and the English in the Middle Ages during the 200-odd years of the Hundred Years War, one of 240 bastides in the southwest of France. Although the

protecting walls here have long been absorbed by newer houses built during more peaceful times, there still remains an air of solid defense behind shuttered windows on the narrow gridworked streets.

In 1395, Vianne, built on the edge of the Baïse River, was already well established and had been for one hundred years. Vianne is the exemplary bastide of the Lot-et-Garonne *département*, with nearly intact walls and an echo of "friend or foe?" still ringing from its towers to its 40-foot walls. Tomorrow we will cross the graceful stone aqueduct over the Baïse River after skipping up the steep double lock called Larderet and Baïse, and moor the *Julia Hoyt* before taking a three-mile ride back to the Middle Ages. Vianne's straight stone walls encircle the village and its gardens with the same sense of protection that must have anchored the thirteenth century when the wall was built to defend Gascony first for the English, later for the French.

Established on Tuesdays some 700 years ago, the summer market now held on Friday evenings recalls the original medieval fairs where animals, wheat, iron, leather, salted fish, and kitchen utensils were traded or sold. What were they going to fix for dinner in 1395? Peacock, swan, whale? Salted meats, preserved greens, and dried fruits also graced medieval larders. Spices from the Indies were used to heighten the flavor of game and birds. Now, merchants with fresh produce or exotic wares from Asia and Africa crowd the Place des Marronniers and impromptu one-night "restaurants" appear in front of butcher shops, storefronts, and normally quiet cafes. The many hundreds of people milling in the usually deserted village square are a reminder of the long heritage of medieval markets and fairs with their important social and commercial aspects. Here, I learn a new recipe for *cornichons...comme grand-mère* or discover a regional variation of goat cheese as I select and buy ripe summer produce before joining friends for dinner at the *escargotlade*—a snail feast sponsored by the local *traiteur* (caterer/deli). The real bustle of this contemporary market is truer to the history of the medieval village than one hundred costumed extravaganzas acted out in châteaus and other tourist destinations.

Buzet-sur-Baïse is our mooring destination for the night. Buzet was built much later than the bastides. Lying between the canal and the Baïse River, Buzet became an important boatyard for the barges that would haul armagnac in casks from further upstream at Condom and barques that carried the rich local wine to Bordeaux. (The Bordeaux wine-growing region extended as far east as Buzet until 1911, but since 1976, the Bordeaux-style wines are called Côtes de Buzet AOC.) Barrel-laden barges shipped liquid goods down the canal to the Garonne River and the docks at Bordeaux's Port de la Demi-Lune.

The bastide church at Vianne

We often stop in Buzet to taste and buy the favored reds and chilled dry rosé wines to replenish the wine cellar of the *Julia Hoyt*.

Monsieur Ryckman opened the door to his *chai* (wine cellar) at the modest Domaine de Versailles at nearby Montignac. The first thing that I saw was a cluster of gauze-shrouded hams suspended overhead. We had come to buy *en vrac* (in bulk) the delicious rustic red Côtes de Buzet that he and his wife produce; it is a favorite on the *Julia Hoyt*. I'll use some to marinate a kilo of beef for a classic daube Gasconne. The wine is full of the character of Southwest France, where wine is thought of more as food than as drink. The old farmhouse kitchen is still fragrant with wood smoke although no fire has burned for some time during the hot summer months. Age-worn Quimper pottery from Monsieur Ryckman's family rests on the crowded mantle; a frozen grandfather clock stands beside the rough-hewn

stone sink built into the kitchen wall, which is still used to wash the tasting glasses. Sitting around the long trestle table weighted by the labeling machine at one end, we taste last year's vintage direct from the barrel.

M. Ryckman regales us with political stories, but lets the wine speak for itself as we walk through a dozen years of sun-washed slopes of gravelly vineyards, tasting back to 1978. When once asked if he aged his wine in wooden barrels, Monsieur Ryckman responded that if we wanted to taste wood, he had a pile of it out in back of the house; if we wanted to taste wine, he would pour us some more from the bottles. As we swirl and look, smell and sip, I daydream of slicing off a slab of that home-cured ham to grill in the fireplace and serve with shallots, a toasted slab of pain de campagne, and a dish of creamy potatoes that have been cooking on the ashes. Reluctantly, I leave the jambon still curing in the grape-scented air as we pack the cases and ten-liter containers of delicious red wine.

Vegetables

Not long before lunchtime, I hear a whisper from the foredeck. "Look, tomatoes ahead!" I pop up from the galley as the *Julia Hoyt* approaches the high stone bridge at Damazan, where, nailed to both sides of the bridge, is a hand-lettered sign announcing "fraises" (strawberries) in June and "tomates" in August. They are red, sweet, and ripe to bursting as only the hot southern French sun can make them.

I don't know her name, the madame who so carefully stakes and weeds the tomato plants along the canal, but I know her pride grows on every stem. We stop to buy four kilos of sweet, acidic tomatoes and she gives us a heavy six kilos. When I ask for three baskets of strawberries, she packs only the very ripest in each basket, then runs to the sprawling plants to pick a few more into a smaller basket *"pour tout de suite"* (for right now). Her pride is as much an advertisement of her gardening art as the tomato-red sweater that she wears on cooler days.

Nowhere are the tomatoes better than in the Garonne Valley in late summer.
I simmer tomato soup, roll out tomato tarts, stuff tomatoes, slice them with shallots and vinegar, make confit of tomatoes, and still we can't get enough. We
cruise by extensive fields of red globes hanging on the vine as the last autumn sun
sweetens the tough-skinned fruit of September. The tomatoes ripening in the
fields will be harvested for tomato paste by October and then we will stir the rich
sun-sweetened tomato magic into sauces, soups, and stews all winter long. Like
my friends and neighbors in the long village, I glean my ideas for dinner not just
from cookbooks but from what is growing in the gardens, offered at the market,
or shared over a neighbor's fence. Although I limit the garden decks on the *Julia
Hoyt* to herbs and flowers, I often share in the long village's harvest. A neighbor

"RUSTIC" WINES OF SOUTHWEST FRANCE

Although overshadowed by their more famous neighbors, the wines of the Southwest are
often as refined as those of Bordeaux. However, the real strength of the regional wines lies in
the diversity of grape varietals that provide a good match for the flavorful Gascon cooking.
The wines of Southwest France are either Bordeaux-style reds of Cabernet Sauvignon,
Cabernet Franc, and Merlot grapes, or they are the eccentric, forgotten grape varietals that
have survived in hidden pockets of the countryside—the Tannats of spicy Madiran and the
Auxerrois or Cot of the black wines of Cahors. Pic Poul and Follie Blanche grapes thrive in the
Armagnac area and are distilled in a distinct manner that retains the character of the soil in
the highly acclaimed and aromatic brandy. We drink dry and sweet white wines of Petit and
Gros Manseng from Pacherenc du Vic Bilh and the Jurançon; fresh dry rosé wines made from
Merlot from the Duras and Marmandais areas. Grown in clay, limestone, or gravel soils, the
vineyards of the Southwest are as varied as the grape varietals.

The wines produced regionally by small vintners and large cooperatives complement
the rustic cuisine and are appreciated and fêted at wine exhibitions throughout France. But
awards are hardly needed to make these wines important to those who enjoy them. Old vines
still worked on family farms are drunk *nouveau* with roasted chestnuts as the year comes to a
close. Engraved and decorated bottles from special years are put aside for future weddings,
baptisms, and celebrations. Dusty green bottles corked by hand age on wire racks alongside
the pâtés and cornichons, jams and confits in the cool and dark stone cellars of village houses.

in her blue-flowered housedress uniform collects a plastic sack of long thin green beans as we chat about the ornate and rusted water pump across from her garden. Passing the beans across the little garden fence hung with blue bursting morning glories, she offers the now familiar admonition that they are "tout naturel." They quickly become incorporated into tonight's dinner as a side dish steamed and tossed with garlic and walnut oil.

Although I'm not always fortunate to stumble on an edible gift, I shop in the same way at the markets, letting the chance encounter with a pile of taut purple-black aubergines or a little wooden crate of *pied du mouton* mushrooms sharpen my senses and influence my menus. I may know what main course I want to prepare when I set off to town, but I often leave the final decision for side dishes and entrées until I see what strikes my fancy; a color, a texture, a certain scent of garden or farm.

I like the French fashion of serving special dishes one at a time in separate courses so I sometimes save these vegetable dishes until after the main course has been served. It's like getting an extra surprise when you thought every plate was on the table. I serve the main course, accompanied only by potatoes (fried, steamed, or au gratin), followed by the separate vegetable course. I enjoy the simple contrasts in textures, flavors, and aromas; the sweet taste of steamed garden vegetables with a home-cured salty ham, a garlicky roast guinea fowl in an armagnac sauce followed by parsnips or celery root purée, a slice of crispy roasted pork with a sharp tossed salad, a baked casserole of vegetables gratinée to serve with a grilled steak and fabulous tomatoes.

GRATIN DE POMMES DE TERRE GRATINÉE
Creamed Baked Potatoes
Serves 4 — 6

From bistro to cafe, restaurant to home, every chef has their own approach to this classic potato dish which is served bubbling and browned hot from the oven. Varying the routine and the ingredients produces subtly different results, but common to all is the need for enough creamy liquid for the potatoes to melt and a long-enough cooking time to allow the magic to happen. Since I am always a little pushed for time in the bistro-galley, I give my gratin a head start by parboiling the peeled potatoes in seasoned milk. After I "slice" the cooked potatoes with a fork to expose more surface area to the cream and heighten the

rough texture, they finish baking in a slow oven as I prepare the rest of my dinner. I always make a generous quantity since this basic "comfort food" always
makes a second round.

2 lb (1 kilo) baking potatoes (about 2
    potatoes per person)
2 cups (16 fl oz/500 ml) milk
1 bay leaf
6 peppercorns
salt
2 cloves garlic, crushed
1 cup (8 fl oz/250 ml) crème fraîche
1/2 teaspoon freshly grated nutmeg
1 cup (4 oz/125 g) grated Gruyère cheese

1. Preheat the oven to 425 degrees F
(220 C).
2. Peel the potatoes and cut in half if
very large. Place in a saucepan and pour
in milk and enough water to cover.
3. Add the bay leaf, peppercorns, and salt to taste, then add the garlic. Cover
the pot and place over medium-high heat until the liquid comes to a rolling
boil. Reduce the heat and simmer the potatoes for fifteen minutes, or until half-
cooked.
4. Drain the potatoes, reserving the liquid. After the potatoes have cooled a
few minutes, "slice" the potatoes with two forks into 3/8-inch (1 cm) slices. In a
greased or nonstick baking pan, place a layer of potatoes, spoon some cream over,
and dust with the grated nutmeg, salt, pepper. Sprinkle one-third of the cheese
over the layer. Repeat two more layers topping with the last of the cheese. Take
the garlic and bay leaf out of the milk and insert them between the layers. Pour
the reserved milk over the potatoes until the liquid just reaches the top layer.
5. Bake for twenty minutes, then reduce the heat to 325 degrees F (165 C)
and continue cooking twenty-five to thirty minutes more.

LES PETITES BILLES
Potato Marbles
Serves 4

In late spring as the first of the new potatoes arrive in the markets with the damp black dirt of the river valley still clinging to them, Patrick gets a sort of "potato fever." The symptoms appear as soon as we arrive at the market at Tonneins or La Reole. Patrick immediately disappears. Within half an hour, he returns to find me somewhere between the poultry and the beets, wearing a 12-year-old's grin on his face. He holds out a lumpy plastic sack and I peer inside to find three or four dozen perfect, tiny, round potatoes the size of marbles. "Lunch!" he declares. "Let's go!" Before I know it, the thin-skinned "marbles" are rolling around a hot pan steaming a little, frying a little, and ready to eat, encrusted with a layer of sea crystals from the Île de Ré. I serve these with almost anything from omelets to duck breasts. But when potato fever strikes, Patrick and the crew will eat the savory bites by themselves.

2 lb (1 kilo) very small new potatoes, red- or white-skinned
1 to 2 tablespoons duck fat, olive oil, or butter
1 tablespoon herbed sea salt (see recipe, page 33)
freshly ground pepper, to taste
1 tablespoon chopped fresh parsley

1. Wash the potatoes but leave their skins on. In a heavy-bottomed frying pan over medium-high heat, place the potatoes, one-half of the fat and 1/2 cup water. Cover tightly.

2. Shake the pan as if you were making popcorn and continue to cook until all the water has evaporated and the potatoes are just tender, about fifteen minutes.

3. Lower the heat and continue cooking with the lid on, shaking the pan from time to time to prevent burning.

4. When the potatoes are done (test by sticking a skewer or fork into one of the largest), toss in the rest of the fat, the sea salt, pepper, and parsley. With the lid off, shake the pan until the potatoes are well covered with the herbs and spices. Use the flat of a large wooden spoon to help the salt adhere to the potato skins if necessary. Keep in a hot oven until ready to serve, or serve immediately.

GALETTE DE POMMES DE TERRE
Crispy Potato Cake
Serves 4

This traditional Gascon galette is cooked in a cast-iron pan over the coals of the hearth until done. However, the stovetop can yield similar results if you take care to use a heavy-bottomed pan. The crispy edges of the cake are a textural punctuation mark to the soft and creamy inside. I like to serve this under a generous helping of Lapin aux Pruneaux.

2 lb (1 kilo) potatoes (Waxy varieties yield different
    results than baking potatoes. Try them both!)
1 tablespoon duck fat or olive oil
salt and freshly ground pepper, to taste
fresly grated nutmeg

    1. Wash, peel, and slice potatoes very thin. Pat dry if very starchy or moist.

    2. In a large sauté pan, spread duck fat or oil, pepper, and nutmeg, and arrange potato slices in a spiral, starting at the center. When the cake is flipped over, this layer is the top, so take care to make it as attractive as possible. Arrange another layer, making sure you use a pan large enough to fit all the potatoes in just two layers.

    3. Place on medium heat and cover, browning slowly. Shake gently from time to time to avoid sticking and wipe the inside of the lid from time to time to keep it dry.

    4. When the bottom layer is well browned, press the potatoes down with a flat spatula, and remove from heat. Place a large plate or platter over the pan and flip it upside down. After checking the pan to make sure it is clean and has enough fat to keep the potato cake from sticking, slide the potato cake, raw-side down, back in the pan to finish cooking. Return to heat, cover, and continue cooking as before.

    5. When done, slide the galette onto a platter, season with salt, and generously cover with a few tablespoons of persillade (see page 134).

PATATES CARAMÉLISÉES
Carmelized Potato Cubes
Serves 4

After a visit to the Musée de Pruneaux (the Prune Museum) on one of my European Culinary Adventures, I took my group of seven eager cooks to lunch in a charming *ferme auberge*, a working farm that caters to adventurous tourists by serving meals prepared on-site using products produced on the farm. A ferme auberge can be the perfect way to sample regional fare if the resident cook, usually the farm wife, is sensitive to her surroundings. On our visit this day, Madame Roy treated us to a "mystery soup" to start our five-course lunch. Only after we'd mopped our bowls with a piece of crusty baguette and encouraged her with satisfied smiles did she disclose that the bright green, creamy *potage mystérieux* was prepared from the very young, knee-high nettles growing by the farmyard fence that enclosed the geese and ducks destined for the farm's foie gras production. We then enjoyed our way through slices of pâté de campagne and a full magret du canard grilled on a wood fire and accompanied by these delicious and slightly sweet golden potato cubes prepared by Madame Roy of the Ferme Auberge de Roussy near Monflanquin. These potatoes should be just slightly sweet, with enough salt and pepper to balance the caramelization. The longer you cook them the better they will taste.

4 large potatoes, peeled and cut in 1-inch (3 cm) cubes
1 tablespoon duck or goose fat, butter, or vegetable oil
1 tablespoon sugar
salt and white pepper

PERSILLADE

This minced parsley and garlic mixture is used to top many different dishes in Southwest France. About one-third garlic to two-thirds parsley, the *persillade* is finely chopped together using a two-handled curved knife on a wooden board. In a country kitchen ritual, young girls are introduced to cooking by learning to make the persillade, and grandmothers rule over the family kitchens by still making the persillade. The flecks of green and white are more than a garnish. Persillade is a serious seasoning and is used generously on steaks, grilled ham, potatoes, and other vegetables. Even *demoiselles* (duck carcasses) are covered with a persillade after they are grilled.

1. Let the cubed potatoes dry on a paper towel or clean dishtowel while you prepare a large frying pan. A nonstick pan works great as long as it has a heavy bottom. Melt the fat in the heavy-bottomed pan over medium-high heat. When the fat is quite hot, put the potato cubes in and reduce the heat to medium. As the potatoes start to brown, turn them on all sides using a set of kitchen tongs or two forks. Remember, there are six sides to a cube so this will take a little time—be patient! Shake the pan to prevent them sticking.

2. When the cubes are half-done, sprinkle the sugar over the remaining surfaces and shake the pan. Continue to cook until all sides are golden brown. Lower the heat and continue cooking, turning as necessary until the potatoes are cooked soft and creamy inside, crispy and crunchy outside. Add salt and pepper, remove from heat, and serve.

LES PETITS NIDS DES PATATES
Little Potato Nests
Serves 4

Like an abandoned bird's nest found on an autumn walk through the forêt de Mas d'Agenais, these twice-cooked potatoes can cradle anything: salt cod and  cornichons, a tiny quail roasting in its own juices, or a savory stew of wild mushrooms picked from the forest floor along the way. A large potato can be a full meal with an accompanying salad and vegetables or the rustic companion to a tasty piece of game or roasted fowl. Choose the potatoes carefully, keeping in mind that you will hollow them out, and need a cavity large enough to accommodate the filling. In the fall, when wild mushrooms are abundant at village markets, I fill these little nests with the following mushroom recipe (inspired by my dear friend Julie) as a main course for lunch or to serve with a slice of home-cured ham.

4 large potatoes
1 clove garlic, unpeeled and crushed with the flat of a knife

Champignons de Julie
Julie's Mushrooms
1 teaspoon duck fat or olive oil
2 shallots, chopped finely
1 lb (500 g) wild and domestic mushrooms: cèpes, chanterelles, pleurotes, morels, oyster mushrooms, or button mushrooms
2 tablespoons red wine vinegar
1 tablespoon whole grain or Dijon mustard
1 teaspoon sugar
1 tablespoon chopped parsley
a sprinkle of fresh chopped herbs: tarragon, thyme, rosemary, sage, or a combination
salt and freshly ground pepper, to taste

1. Preheat the oven to 425 degrees F (220 C). Bring a pot of salted water to boil and prepare a lightly-oiled roasting pan.

2. Leaving the skins on the potatoes, slice off a thin lid from one side. With a spoon or a melon baller, remove enough of the flesh to create a hollow for the filling. Reserve the potato flesh to one side. Add the garlic clove and the hollowed-out potatoes to the boiling water. Bring back to a boil and cook for five to ten minutes, or until the potatoes start to get soft. Don't overcook or they will fall apart in the water! When done drain upside down.

3. Place the fat and the chopped shallots in a saucepan over medium heat. Chop the large mushrooms in big chunks, leaving small mushrooms whole, and place in the pan as the shallots start to soften and go translucent. Stir until the mushrooms are lightly coated with the fat and starting to give off their juices.

4. Add the vinegar and mustard and continue cooking until a velvety sauce is made. (If needed, add a little wine to extend the sauce.) Stir in the parsley, herbs, sugar, salt, and pepper.

5. Spoon the mixture into the potato shells and place the stuffed potatoes in the roasting pan.

6. Chop or grate some of the reserved potato bits into small, fine shreds and toss with salt, herbs, and pepper. Place a little heap of this "nesting material" on top of the filling.

7. Bake for thirty minutes or until the potato is completely cooked, the filling is bubbling hot, and the potato shreds on top are crispy. Serve hot with a roasted pintade or wild game.

ÉTOUFFADE DE POMMES DE TERRE
Smothered Potatoes
Serves 4 — 6

These slow-cooked potatoes steam in their own savory moisture and are flavored by the familiar salty ventreche, sweet shallots, onions, and thyme. As
Vetou Pompèle stirs a big pot of the smothered potatoes on her crowded stove,
the edges of the floury baking potatoes break up and mash together with the
savory bits, and the consistency becomes a cross between crispy sautéed bites
and steamed mashed potatoes. Choose russets or the creamier Yukon Gold potatoes and serve with a roast pork loin or grilled meats. If your timing is off, these
will keep well in a warm oven covered with aluminum foil; remove the foil ten
minutes before serving.

8 potatoes
2 tablespoons duck fat or olive oil
2 onions, chopped
2 shallots, chopped
4 oz (125 g) ventreche, bacon, or salted ham
1 teaspoon fresh chopped thyme
1 bay leaf
1 tablespoon all-purpose flour
1 cup (8 fl oz / 250 ml) chicken broth or water
salt and freshly ground pepper, to taste
1 tablespoon chopped parsley

1. Peel and cut the potatoes into large chunks.

2. In a heavy-bottomed covered pot, heat the fat over medium heat. Add the
chopped onions and shallots, the ventreche, bacon, or ham, thyme, and bay leaf.
Stir and let cook about ten minutes. Sprinkle the flour over the mixture and stir
until brown.

3. Add the potato chunks, broth or water, and salt and pepper. Mix well
with a wooden spoon. Cover the casserole and let cook slowly about forty-five
minutes, stirring often to keep it from sticking.

4. Serve on a warm plate and garnish with the chopped parsley.

OIGNONS CONFITURE
Red Onion Relish
Serves 4—6

This intensely flavored vegetable side dish is a favorite on the *Julia Hoyt* when I serve it with grilled chicken or lamb chops. This confit may be served hot or at room temperature as a relish with roasts and fowl. It will keep in the refrigerator for several days.

1 tablespoon olive oil
1 lb (500 g) red onions, sliced
   very thin
1 tablespoon sugar
2 tablespoons red wine vinegar
   or balsamic vinegar
salt and freshly ground pepper, to taste
2 tablespoons dried fruit
   (raisins, apricots, figs,
   prunes), chopped
1/2 cup (4 oz/60 ml) red wine

1. Heat oil in noncorrosive saucepan over medium heat. Add onions. Let sweat gently until onions start to give off their juices.

2. Stir in sugar, vinegar, salt, and pepper until the mixture starts to melt. Add dried fruit and wine, then cover and reduce heat to lowest setting. Use a heat diffuser on the burner, if necessary. Watch and stir often, adding more wine or water as needed.

3. When the onions and fruit have melded and cooked down to a jamlike consistency, taste and adjust seasoning. Add more vinegar if needed to balance the fruit.

Note: I stuff a tablespoon of this onion "jam" in small, hollow parboiled onions and roast them in the oven.

PURÉE DE CÉLERI-RAVE
Celery Root Purée
Serves 4

After I had been cruising and cooking in my long village for a year, a barge-guest gave me Paula Wolfert's definitive *The Cooking of South-West France*. Not only did I discover the answers to so many of my regional culinary questions, but I found this lighter version of a traditional celery root purée. Here, an apple replaces the usual potato. I like how the celery and apple flavors imperceptibly blend, and I seldom need to add butter, cream, or crème fraîche to have a smooth-textured purée. This is my favorite way to serve celery root to first-time guests on the *Julia Hoyt*.

1 celery root, trimmed, peeled, and chopped
1 apple, peeled and chopped
1 quart (1 liter) nonfat milk
1 tablespoon butter, optional
salt and white pepper
freshly grated nutmeg

   1. Place celery root and apple in a saucepan. Cover with milk and simmer over low heat until soft, approximately twenty to thirty minutes. Remove from heat and strain, reserving the liquid.

   2. Purée the cooked celery root and apple in a food processor or ricer using a little of the reserved liquid as needed. Blend in the butter, if desired, season with salt and pepper, and garnish with nutmeg. Serve warm with a garnish of celery leaves.

PURÉE DE CHÂTAIGNES
Chestnut Purée
Serves 4

My dear friend Annie loves the sweetened chestnut purée that comes in toothpaste-type tubes or is canned in miniature tins with heavily decorated labels. Whenever I return from France, I have several tubes in my suitcases for this esoteric sweet tooth. But in my long village, chestnuts are the signal of a different type of treat.

In autumn, when the new wine is distributed at village markets still bubbling and foaming from antique wooden casks, there are always chestnuts roasting over makeshift grills. When the first game of fall is caught and spit-roasted over the fire, there are boiled or baked chestnuts to scald your chilled fingertips. For this chestnut purée, I bicycle down the towpath past the first lock at Bruch and spot the few remaining wild chestnut trees that litter the path with shiny flat nuts. I serve just a couple of tablespoons of this rich and creamy purée with a roasted pheasant or a joint of *sanglier* (wild boar). The purée can be presented prettily on a golden October leaf, in a tiny mushroom "basket," or spread on a couple of slices of oven-roasted bread.

1 lb (500 g) fresh chestnuts
1 star anise
1 bay leaf
1 onion, chopped finely
1 tablespoon sweet butter
2 to 3 tablespoons crème fraîche or heavy cream
salt and white pepper, to taste

1. Score a cross in each chestnut with the tip of a knife. Place the chestnuts, the star anise, and the bay leaf in a pot of boiling water. Let boil for ten to fifteen minutes until the chestnuts are easy to peel and cooked thoroughly.

2. Peel the chestnuts and break them up with a fork.

3. Place the onion in a heavy-bottomed sauté pan with the butter. Cook slowly over a low heat until the onion is soft and translucent.

4. Place the chestnuts and the onion in a food processor and purée, adding the cream. If the chestnuts are very dry, add a little broth or a couple of tablespoons of port or sherry until you have a stiff but smooth purée. Return to the heat and warm over a low flame, taking care not to burn.

5. To keep the purée warm, put it in a bowl covered with aluminum foil and place the bowl in a pan of hot water up to the halfway mark of the bowl.

POIREAUX BRAISÉS
Braised Leeks
Serves 4

Grabbing several bunches of leeks at the morning markets is like buying insurance; insurance that all through the week the mild oniony flavor will perfume soups and tourtes and take a starring role in dinner one night. Braised leeks melt into a false butteriness to flatter a roast beef or a baked herb-crusted chicken.

6 fresh leeks
1 cup (8 fl oz/250 ml) white wine
1 cup (8 fl oz/250 ml) vegetable or chicken broth or
    water
1 tablespoon olive oil
salt, to taste
1 fresh lemon, optional

1. Clean and trim the leeks, leaving just the white part and the first hint of light green. To clean of all sandy grit, slice the leeks in 2- to 3-inch (8 cm) pieces and soak in a bowl of warm water, washing them gently with your hands. Place the trimmed and cut leeks in the bottom of a covered saucepan or deep frying pan.

2. Pour the wine, broth or water, olive oil, and salt over the leeks and place on medium-low heat. Cover and cook slowly for fifteen to twenty minutes until the leeks are tender.

3. Remove the lid and reduce the liquid until there is approximately 1/2 cup of liquid left.

4. Serve the leeks with some of the juice poured over and a squeeze of lemon juice, if desired.

Eglise des vignes after the harvest

CRÊPES DE COURGETTES
Zucchini Crêpes
Serves 4

In the middle of summer when French gardens are overflowing their neatly trimmed borders, I am always offered a *panier* of tomatoes, a *sac* of sweet peas, or a *boîte* of young tender zucchini. Picked when small, courgettes have a sweetness that is easily masked and too often cooked out. This simple recipe allows the flavor of the zucchini to perfume the crêpe batter and shows off their slightly firm texture. As a companion to a fan of sliced duck breasts or to a slice of grilled ham served with shallots and vinegar, these green-speckled crêpes are at their best served hot and dusted with a couple of grinds of fresh pepper.

4 small zucchini (courgettes), coarsely grated
    (including skin)
1/4 cup (1 oz/35 g) all-purpose flour
2 eggs
1 tablespoon oil
1/4 teaspoon salt
freshly ground pepper

1. Squeeze out some of the excess moisture by placing the grated zucchini (courgettes) in a few paper towels. Roll up the towels and press until most of the moisture is absorbed.

2. In a medium bowl, combine the flour and eggs. Beat furiously with a wooden spoon until you have a thick, smooth paste. Beat in the oil and salt. Stir in the grated zucchini until all is mixed together well and the zucchini is coated with the batter mixture.

3. Heat a heavy-bottomed skillet or griddle over a medium-high heat and brush with a light coat of oil to keep the crêpes from sticking. Drop large spoonfuls of the batter on the griddle and cook until lightly browned, then turn and brown the other side.

4. Remove the crêpes as they are done to a warm platter and keep them hot in a warm oven until ready to serve. Sprinkle them with freshly ground pepper before serving.

HARICOTS VERTS À LA CAMPAGNE
Country-style Green Beans
Serves 4

A mountain of *haricots verts* is heaped on a hot platter and placed on the oil-cloth-covered kitchen table. A plump chicken is jointed by the kitchen sink. Before the chicken arrives at its place of honor for this Sunday lunch in Gascony, we dive into the green beans, passing them around. Steaming and juicy in a garlic-infused "sauce," this classic French vegetable is nearly a meal in itself. We eat a helping of beans, then pass the chicken, then eat *more* beans. There is a healthy luxury in the abundance of the bountiful harvests from a garden that yields baskets and baskets of thin green legumes. Translate this bounty to your table and serve haricots verts to fill a heaping salad plate per person.

1 lb (500 g) very fresh thin green beans
1/2 teaspoon salt
2 ripe tomatoes, skinned and chopped
2 cloves garlic, peeled and crushed
1 tablespoon walnut oil (Make sure nut oils are fresh. They have a short shelf life and can easily go rancid sitting opened on your kitchen shelf. Buy them in small quantities and remember to use them in salad dressings!)
1 teaspoon chopped fresh tarragon, optional
salt and freshly ground pepper, to taste

1. After trimming the tops and tails of the beans, place in a large pot of boiling salted water. Cook until half-done, about ten minutes. (For me "done" means quite done. I like the texture and flavor of tender well-cooked beans; for Patrick they would be barely warm and snap crisply between the teeth! Cook to your taste.)

2. Drain the water from the pot and add the chopped tomatoes and garlic cloves. Cover and let cook ten minutes more or to your liking.

3. Add the walnut oil, tarragon, and salt and pepper. Serve hot, or cover and let sit until almost ready to serve, then reheat briefly.

CAROTTES GLACÉ AU VIN DE ROSÉ
Carrots Glazed with Rosé Wine

"What's wrong these these carrots? They're so orange!" That was my nephew Mike, on a summer visit to the *Julia Hoyt*. At seventeen, Mike was already an able sous-chef, but the fresh from the garden sweetness of the French produce continued to surprise him as it does all my city slicker friends. It is worthwhile to seek out farmers markets and greengrocers that monitor their produce and taste the carrots to make sure they are fresh, sweet, and flavorful. Buy only enough carrots for a few days and don't refrigerate the life (and moisture) out of them. Instead, use one of those lovely baskets cluttering your cupboards and display the produce on a countertop.

I like to "wash" these carrots with a simple sauce when they are half-cooked and let them steep in the fruity but dry local rosé wine. It is a technique I use over and over in the bistro-galley. I partially cook my vegetables and then, leaving them covered, I let them rest until I am ready to finish the meal. This frees up an extra burner on the stove, keeps them from overcooking, and allows me to have all of my meal hot and ready at the same time.

1 lb (500 g) fresh carrots
1 cup (8 fl oz/240 ml) dry rosé wine or dry white wine
1 sprig fresh rosemary
1 leaf verveine (lemon verbena is sold as an herb tea)
1 tablespoon sweet butter

1. Peel and trim the carrots, leaving them whole if not too large, or cut them in 3-inch (8 cm) lengths. Put the carrots in a lidded saucepan and barely cover with water. Cook covered for ten to fifteen minutes over medium-high heat.

2. Drain the water and add the wine, rosemary, and lemon verbena. Lower the heat to low and continue cooking. When the carrots are almost done, cover and let sit for five minutes or until ready to serve.

3. To serve the carrots, add butter, return to high heat, uncovered, and reduce the wine almost completely. Do not brown the carrots. Gently shake the carrots in the sauce until they are glazed. Serve hot with a garnish of fresh lemon verbena or mint.

STE. COLOMBE-EN-BRUILHOIS

The End of the Journey

HOMEPORT. THE END of our voyage; the beginning of new adventures. Unfurling the heavy mooring lines with a great heave to the towpath is like slipping off your shoes after a long day, home again. The last straight stretch of canal that leads to Camont, our homeport, is lined by poplar trees special to this end of the long village. The *Julia Hoyt* glides through this leafy green tunnel past familiar farms and faces to reach Ste. Colombe-en-Bruilhois.

A trinity of old villages, Serignac-sur-Garonne, Brax, and Ste. Colombe-en-Bruilhois, are our last ports of call on the long village. Their histories are long, reaching back before the Romans through the early Middle Ages, surviving the Hundred Years War, the religious wars, the French Revolution, and the coming of the modern age with the *chemin de fer* (the railroad) and the automobile. From the dominating view of Ste. Colombe at the top of the valley's south ridge to the riverside orchards of the Garonne, this is the last rural respite before the canal stair-steps up four imposing locks to the Pont Canal d'Agen, the 534-meter-long (1,725 feet) aqueduct that crosses the Garonne at the entrance to the busy city.

This is the end of my long village but it's not the end of the canal. The Canal Latéral à la Garonne will continue to rise gently for another 100 kilometers before spilling into the junction of the Canal du Midi at Toulouse. There are more towns of interest and charm—Agen, Valence d'Agen, and Moissac. The fruitful orchards at the confluence of the Tarn and

The pigeonnier at Camont

Monsieur Dupuy, mushroom hunter

Garonne rivers give way to the clickity-clack industry of small factory works built beside the railroad tracks running parallel to the canal and into Toulouse.

Each small community here at homeport offers us a different aspect of daily life. Serignac and Brax are the centers of commerce along the two-lane departmental road; bakeries, butchers, épiceries, tobacconists and newspaper stalls, post offices, and hotels propose all the necessities of village life. By contrast, Ste. Colombe-en-Bruilhois sits near heaven, four kilometers away on the top of the ridge, and affords little else besides silence and a spectacular view of La Garonne as she weaves her way into the city of Agen. The purity of this now quiet village is reflected in the just-scrubbed stone steeple of the Église de Notre Dame, a lesson in Roman, Byzantine, and Gothic architecture. Ste. Colombe-en-Bruilhois is our special village, our address.

The Bruilhois, once an extensive wild wooded area, reached all the way to the Garonne River, and Ste. Colombe claimed a strip of river frontage from which to launch goods to market, as did most hill towns of its age. Ste. Colombe was found-

The faded blue doors of La Source

ed in 900 A.D., a tribute to the virgin martyr Colombe, a local cult figure. It sported three religious centers, including a medieval hospice for women at Goulard. It is still possible to imagine the hundreds of thousands of pilgrims on the long road to the tomb of Saint Jacques de Compostelle in western Spain stopping to take solace in benevolent Ste. Colombe. It retains this aura of calm and tranquil retreat as we pull in to take our safe haven beneath the poplar trees.

Camont, a cluster of late-eighteenth-century farm buildings in the center of this triangle of small villages, is our homeport. It is here that the *Julia Hoyt* comes to rest and hook up to the umbilical cords of water, power, and mooring lines. Built just after the French Revolution, Camont is a layercake of stone, rubble, and brick. The Garonne contributed the river rock which was sandwiched between flat "Roman" bricks to build the 1-meter-thick walls. This typical Gascon farm ages crookedly under a pretty jumble of red tile roofs: the long barn divided by solid elm cattle stalls, the *cave* that houses two huge wine vats, and the three-tiered pigeonnier crowned by a couple of yellow confit pots as rural decoration.

The first person I met at Camont was Monsieur Dupuy. We bought the former farm of Madame and Monsieur Dupuy, inheriting them as neighbors and friends. Now they live across the lane in a modern bungalow. For the last fifty years Monsieur Dupuy has walked daily to the spring to tend the watercress and collect water. He fetches spring water for soup from "*la fontaine,*" as he calls it, or hunts the fragile white mushrooms called *peupliers* which grow at the base of the poplar trees. In his battered pith helmet or stocking hat, depending on the season, he walks the paths to the wooded site, stick and jug over his shoulder, and maintains his prior ownership over this old farm. The area where he used to run the dairy cows from the *crémerie* along the towpath and between the trees is now overgrown with weeds and bramble.

Fresh water flows by our doors at Camont. The canal is just steps away but more important to the life of the farm is *la source*, the freshwater spring. The spring supplies pure water for a dozen neighbors who regularly fill their containers at the simple pipe jammed into the hillside. Important to the farming community in times of drought and now in times of chemical-saturated wells, the spring is the source for more than just the cool clear water that some say comes from the Pyrenees, many miles away. Laundry has been washed, children have been bathed, soup has been made, and gardens have been fed with the hallowed water.

Born at Camont, Madame Dupuy remembers its canal-related history and tells the story of how at the turn of the century, her parents hopped a ride on a barge to Toulouse for their honeymoon. Sitting in the shade one day, she told me how for her own wedding she walked the three kilometers down the little dirt lane to Brax wearing her white gown and veil. She and her *jeune homme*, Monsieur Dupuy, made their vows then to live beside the long village for the rest of their lives. The lane, though still narrow, is paved now, and fast trucks full of gravel from a new quarry roar past the nearly sleeping farm.

I listen to these stories as if watching a romantic soft-focus film, the wrinkles of everyday life defused by time and distance. I hunt for souvenirs of those early days hidden in the shutter-darkened rooms: a nail in a beam from which a ham hung; a dried lamb's tail once used to grease some rusting tools; an iron pot worn thin from incessant stirring.

*Fetching water from
la fontaine*

The distinctive pigeonnier at Camont is a landmark along the canal. Throughout Southwest France we see pigeonniers of all types—square or round, freestanding or attached, as porches and turrets, half-timbered or cut-stone. Valued for their individual designs, they have become the focus of regional restoration efforts. From the arched window on the second floor of Camont's pigeonnier, its beams blackened by wood fires and hung with woven nesting baskets, I can almost see phantom barges of the nineteenth century passing, pulled by sullen oxen or pairs of sturdy horses. The four rows of poplar trees hold the last hundred years within their breezy foliage.

I call our pile of stones *"le relais aux longs jours,"* the inn of the long days, because of its history as a watering and rest stop and relay point for the barges. The horsemen whose teams hauled the fully loaded barges from sunup to after nightfall were called *"charretiers aux longs jours"*—carters of the long days. Barge owners too poor to afford their own animals would rent these carters' services from village to village all the way to Castets-en-Dorthe. In summer when night doesn't fall until after 11 p.m., there are still very long days at Camont.

We all have our touchstones somewhere, even boat gypsies, and the herb garden at Camont is mine. The flower-strewn beds are edged with old wine bottles. The mosaic terra-cotta path leads to a circle of painted metal garden chairs on the thyme-hedged gravel terrace. In the long twilight of midsummer, when friends outnumber the crew, we spill off the decks of the *Julia Hoyt*, onto the towpath, and into the garden. This is where we hang the Chinese lanterns and barbecue.

The little farm I garden at predates the canal by over sixty years. Although its dairy cows no longer graze along the towpath trees and cross the nearest bridge to reach the riverside fields, and its aproned farm wives who offered hospitality and board to passing bargemen are but a tintype memory, I keep its rustic kitchen open.

In the large open kitchen at Camont the massive square nail that hangs on the inside of the fireplace mantle once supported a *"dinde à la ficelle,"* a turkey on a string, for Madame Dupuy's *fête de mariage*, trussed and roasting over a copper pan layered with slabs of bread to collect the succulent drippings. The lean bird would be rubbed with the moppings to baste the skin with savory juices and the bread would accompany the meat at the feast. The *crémaillère*, the heavy notched hook on the back wall, can still hold a heavy pot full of plump rabbits and plums stewing in wine. The black andirons support a giant *brochette* on which ducks and chickens, quail, or a dozen little birds can still be turned to a crispy gold as the room warms to the glowing coals.

My European Culinary Adventures always focus around the hearth and this eccentric old kitchen at Camont. We learn to cook the rustic recipes in this high-ceilinged room where the potatoes were once stored, where hams were hung from the beams, and fires were lit to boil the water for the yearly *fête de cochon* (pig butchering celebration) preparations. Pots fly between the bistro-galley and the hearth and my students wander from kitchen to terrace, where we set up tables and I share stories told to me of life on this wonderful forgotten farm.

DESSERT

The journey through the long village ends as sweetly as dinner ends, with fruit and creams and short pastry tarts. In this area, desserts are rarely too sugary or bloated with heavy creams. More often than not, some summer fruits are simmered in a light wine syrup, a clean spoon custard is aromatized with verveine (lemon verbena) from the garden and richly yellow with eggs. Armagnac is splashed around the inside of a buttery tart and dusted with sugar, or black and

bitter chocolate is paired with tangy crème fraîche and poured in a little pot to spoon rich and melting in the mouth. Like the rest of the rustic and rural cuisine of Gascony, the refinement in the desserts comes from the subtle combination of flavors and textures presented in a straightforward way. Cutting a crisp papery tarte de pomme washed with a combination of orange flower water, zest, and eau-de-vie and served alongside a steaming cup of black coffee is a fitting salute to the end of a journey that began with aperitifs a week—or was it a lifetime—ago.

In my long village, in the days when horses still pulled the barges, the soup plate once again was mopped clean with a bit of bread and this time turned upside down. The dessert was served on the back of the plate. At homeport, we honor the sweet finish with specially decorated Limoges *porcelaine* or other fancy plates, souvenirs of another time.

TARTE AUX POMMES
French Apple Tart
Makes one 10-inch (25 cm) tart

I remember...and dream of sugar-dusted pastry layered with thin slices of perfectly ripe fruit—the quintessential French fruit tart. If it's summer, I layer the most fragrant strawberries over a bed of creamy yellow custard or slice two giant peaches dripping onto a crust that is washed with egg yolk and powdered with coarse sugar. In autumn, we collect the sharp, sweet apples from the long-neglected orchard at Camont and bake a rustic tarte aux pommes, letting the buttery crust drape over the apple slices and edge the topless pie. And if friends drop by the *Julia Hoyt* and stay, as they often do, for hours of contented conversation, I talk from the bistro-galley while I prepare a papery crust dusted with perfumed sugar—a delicious *tarte au sucre.*

This recipe can be modified to use almost any fruit, but take the care to choose only what is in season and perfectly ripe. Think of these pastry tarts as making "jam in a crust," bubbling, sweet, and perfumed with orchard and garden.

Pâte Brisée Sucrée
Sweet Short Pastry Crust
Makes pastry for one 10-inch (25 cm) tart pan.

1 cup (4 oz/125 g) flour
1 tablespoon sugar
1/4 cup (2 oz/60 g) butter
1/4 cup (2 fl oz/60 ml) water

1. Place the flour and the sugar in a mixing bowl. Add the butter, broken up into small bits. Work the butter into the flour with your fingertips until the whole is crumbly and even-textured, like cornmeal. (Alternately, use a food processor or hand tool.)

2. Stir in half of the water and mix quickly, adding just enough more water to make the dough hold together. Pat the dough into a ball with your hands. Let the dough rest while you prepare the filling.

3. Divide dough in half. Roll out the dough until 1/8 inch (3 mm) thick and lay in pan. Fill and bake the pastry shell or bake *blanc* (empty) using pastry weights or beans.

1 short pastry crust
2 lb (1 kilo) apples, peeled, cored, and sliced 1/4 inch (5 mm) thick
1/4 cup (2 fl oz/60 ml) armagnac (or brandy, rum, or calvados)
1/4 cup (2 oz/60 g) sugar
1 teaspoon vanilla sugar
crème fraîche

1. Preheat oven to 425 degrees F (220 C).
2. Sprinkle the apple slices with the armagnac or other liquor and sugar. Set aside.
3. Prepare the pastry and line the tart pan. Flute the edges prettily.
4. Place the apples in a spiral or just neatly in the bottom of the pastry shell.
5. Bake for twenty-five to thirty minutes until done.
6. Sprinkle the vanilla sugar over the surface of the apples and place beneath the oven's broiler until caramelized. Let cool and serve with a dollop of crème fraîche on the side.

TARTE D'ÉTÉ À LA CRÈME
Summer Fruit Custard Tart
Makes one 10-inch (25 cm) tart

The pretty windows of the pâtisseries in the villages along the canal look like jewelry stores. Spotless showcases are filled with shallow tarts covered with glistening fruit. Ruby hearts of strawberries, garnets of whole raspberries, kiwi emeralds, and topaz apricots and peaches adorn prebaked pastry crusts layered with a rich egg cream. It is this *crème pâtissière* that bonds the juicy fruit and provides a custardy base for each sweet bite. Then a shiny glaze of homemade apricot *gelée* is washed across the filling and set to chill until Sunday dinner. Although I often bring home one of these treats from my village expeditions, I like to make these easy individual "jewel" tarts for the friends cruising with us when the summer fruit orchards are overflowing. It's as easy as 1, 2, 3, 4...

1. Pastry Crust

Preheat the oven to 425 degrees F (220 C). Make a pastry crust (see recipe, pages 152-153) and line a shallow tart pan; one with a removable bottom plate is preferable. If making individual tarts, use 3-inch (8 cm) tart pans, dividing the pastry into golf ball-sized pieces. Flute the edges of the crust to make a little lip. Prick the pastry with a fork and place dry beans or pastry weights in the pans and bake for fifteen to twenty minutes. The pastry should be very light golden. Let cool and remove pastry weights.

2. Crème Pâtissière

2-inch (5 cm) piece vanilla bean
1 cup (8 fl oz/250 ml) milk
2 egg yolks
1/4 cup (2 oz/60 g) sugar
1/4 cup (1 oz/30 g) all-purpose flour

Place the vanilla bean in the milk and bring to a slow boil over medium heat. Be careful not to let the milk boil over or scorch. Remove from the heat and let cool as the vanilla bean infuses the milk. Beat the egg yolks and the sugar with a whisk until the mixture is light yellow and flows smoothly from the whisk in ribbons. Sift the flour into the egg mixture and beat until smooth. Add some of the tepid milk to the egg mixture little by little. Remove the vanilla bean. Add the egg mixture to the rest of the milk after removing the vanilla bean and return to a very low heat. Cook three to five minutes, stirring constantly until the cream thickens to a dense pudding. Remove from the heat and let cool completely, stirring often to keep a skin from forming, or place a piece of plastic wrap on the surface. When cool, spread a half-inch (15 mm) layer on the bottom of the pie shell.

3. Fruit Layer
2 lb (1 kilo) assorted fresh fruit; strawberries, raspberries, kiwis, apricots, peaches, or grapes

Prepare the fruit by handling as little as possible and wash or wipe carefully. With strawberries, remove the stems. Leave some small ones whole; slice the rest into little fans. Slice apricots in half and pit them. Peel and slice kiwis. Stone peaches. Arrange on the custard layer in a pretty fashion; one apricot half, a couple of strawberry fans, and a kiwi slice will cover a small 3-inch tart. Or cover the entire surface with whole raspberries placed in concentric circles, stem end down into the cream.

4. Apricot Glaze
1 cup (8 oz/250 ml) high-quality apricot jam
1 tablespoon armagnac

Place a small jar (8 oz/250 ml) of apricot jam in a small saucepan and cook over low heat. When the jam has liquified, strain through a sieve or colander to remove any fruit pulp and return to the pan. Add 1 tablespoon armagnac or other fruit brandy or liqueur and bring to a boil. Remove from heat, let the glaze cool slightly, and brush over the fruit. Chill before serving.

TARTE AUX POIRE ET CHOCOLAT
Pear and Chocolate Tart
Makes one 10-inch (25 cm) tart

Especially for chocolate lovers, this is a chocolaty twist on a French fruit tart. Make this tart when pears are ripe and juicy, or use pear halves that have been preserved in syrup. If using canned pears, stir a little of the syrup into the final cream. This is a great combination of delicate pear flavor enhanced by the pear eau-de-vie and rich dark chocolate bound by a creamy liaison and served in a crusty shell.

1 recipe sweet short pastry dough (see pages 152-153)
8 oz (250 g) sweet, dark chocolate
1 cup (8 fl oz/250 ml) crème fraîche
3 large ripe pears, peeled and halved (canned pears work well too)
1 egg
1/2 teaspoon pure vanilla extract
2 tablespoons Poire William (pear brandy or liqueur)
granulated sugar

   1. Preheat the oven to 425 degrees F (220 C).
   2. Prepare the pastry and line the tart pan.
   3. Melt the chocolate over very low heat or in a double boiler. Stir in about 3 tablespoons of crème fraîche.
   4. Spread the chocolate mixture evenly over the pastry.
   5. Core the pear halves with a spoon or melon baller, then slice them into fans by cutting lengthwise from the bottom almost to the top of the pear, stopping 1 inch (3 cm) from the top. Fan the pears over the chocolate and place in a circle around the pan. Bake for twenty minutes. Remove from oven, but keep oven on.

6. Mix remaining crème fraîche, egg, vanilla, and Poire William together. Pour around the pears, covering the chocolate. Sprinkle with sugar. Return to the hot oven and bake until golden or place under a broiler for a few minutes. Let cool and serve.

TARTE AU SUCRE
Sugar Tart
Makes one 10-inch (25 cm) tart

This is the simplest of all pastry desserts. Clotilde's mother, Melinda, showed me how to fold the buttery crust over itself and the sugary filling. I have since made it often as an impromptu dessert on the *Julia Hoyt* when an afternoon tea party is in session. It reminds me of the bits of leftover pastry that my mother would let us shape and sprinkle with sugar to burn in the oven. Use only pastry that you have made from scratch or the highest-quality readymade pastry that you can find; the simpler the dish, the more important it is that its ingredients be the best. This tart is flaky and sweet, best served warm.

1 recipe sweet short pastry dough (see pages 152-153)
1 egg
1 jigger armagnac or rum
1 handful granulated sugar mixed with some vanilla sugar

1. Preheat the oven to 425 degrees F (220 C). Prepare a 10-inch (25 cm) tart pan.
2. Roll out the pastry 3 inches (8 cm) larger than the pan. Place the pastry in the tart pan, letting the leftover part drape over the edges.
3. Beat the egg and armagnac or rum together in a small bowl. Use enough of this mixture to brush the entire surface of the pastry using a pastry brush.
4. Sprinkle the pastry generously with most of the sugar.
5. Fold over the edges of the pastry, enclosing the sugar in a sort of rustic envelope. Brush this newly exposed surface with the rest of the egg wash and sprinkle with the remaining sugar. Bake in a hot oven for twenty to twenty-five minutes until golden brown and crispy. Serve warm.

PRUNES JACOTS
Plum Packets ·

In French, a *prune* is a plum and *pruneaux* are prunes. In this fresh plum recipe, the sugar plum packets are great eaten warm from a bowl with a spoonful of cream poured over. They can be taken on a *pique-nique* to be eaten out of hand. The cinnamon-sugar mixture that I spoon into each cavity melts with the fruit juices and can make a sweet sticky mess on the pan. So be sure to line the cookie pan with aluminum foil or use a nonstick pan. The kids of Camont, Grace, Thom, and Clotilde, love these sweet packets in crusty sugar-dusted jackets. I use, of course, the plums of Agen, *prune d'Ente*, grown for drying and full of sugar when ripe and fresh. But ripe greengage and little mirabelle plums work too.

double recipe sweet short pastry dough (see pages 152-153)
12 ripe plums, purple or green
1/2 cup (4 oz/125 g) plus 1 tablespoon sugar
1 teaspoon ground cinnamon
1/4 teaspoon freshly ground nutmeg
1/4 cup (2 oz/60 g) butter, cut into 12 bits
1 egg, beaten

1. Preheat the oven to 425 degrees F (220 C).

2. Roll the pastry out onto a board and cut into 12 equal 4-inch (10 cm) squares.

3. Pit the plums by cutting an "X" into the top and removing the pit with a knife or a small spoon.

4. Combine the sugar and spices in a bowl.

5. Place one plum over a pastry square and spoon a little of the sugar mixture into the fruit's cavity. (It doesn't matter if some of the sugar spills onto the dough.) Push a bit of butter into the cavity to make a "plug."

6. Pull the pastry up around the plum on all sides, making a pouch that is sealed at the top. Pinch the edges together well and then seal by brushing the beaten egg over the top. Sprinkle with some of the remaining sugar.

7. Place on an aluminum foil-lined cookie sheet or in a muffin tin and bake until golden brown, about twenty-five minutes. Remove from oven and let cool or serve warm with cream or *crème anglaise* (see page 160).

GRATIN DES DEUX PÊCHES
Two-Peach Gratin
Serves 4 — 6

There is a brief time, in the middle of summer, when both the fragrant white peaches with their rosy blushed skins and the heavy sweet yellow peaches are available at the corner farm. Madame Sabadini will call me to come pick up a juice-stained wooden box of peaches when I am in homeport. The hand-lettered sign on the road announces *"fruit à la ferme"* and most of the perfect fruit has been sold to village folk driving back from an afternoon's shopping in Agen. But there are still dozens of imperfect bird-pecked or bruised peaches left. I reserve the best for peeling and poaching in a champagne syrup and slice a few for a two-colored gratin using crème fraîche. The rest I peel and chop into a small copper kettle, a boat-sized miniature of my neighbor's caldron-sized vats, for making a peach compote, or a quick confiture for early-morning croissants. The peaches in this fruit gratin can be replaced by nearly any very ripe and juicy fruit with great success.

1 tablespoon butter
2 lb (1 kilo) peaches: 1/2 white peaches, 1/2 yellow peaches, peeled and sliced
1/4 cup (2 oz/60 g) sugar
1 tablespoon orange zest
orange flower water
1 cup (8 fl oz/250 ml) crème fraîche or heavy (double) cream
1 egg

   1. Preheat the oven to 425 degrees F (220 C). Butter an oven-proof casserole dish.
   2. Place the two different peach slices in two different bowls. Sprinkle the sugar (reserving two teaspoons), orange zest, and a couple of dashes of orange flower water over each bowl. Turn over with a spoon until all the slices are coated.
   3. In a small bowl, mix the cream and the egg together.
   4. Place the slices in alternate bands of color in the gratin pan. Pour the egg/cream mixture over the top. Sprinkle with a couple of teaspoons of sugar and place in the hot oven. Bake for twenty-five to thirty minutes or until the peach juice is bubbling and the cream browns on the top. Serve warm with a shortbread cookie or other crispy biscuit.

POIRES BANDELLO
Poached Pears with Poire William Custard Sauce
Serves 4

Pears poached in wine is a standard in many restaurants these days. In my long village, where the good local rosé wine is dry and fruity, I like to tint the pears pink as they poach and serve them with a pale crème anglaise (custard sauce) perfumed with Monsieur Gros' exquisite Poire William eau-de-vie inspired by the poet Bandello. Choose ripe but firm pears that are small and full of flavor like those grown on the hills of the Garonne Valley.

CRÈME ANGLAISE (CUSTARD SAUCE)

2 cups (16 fl oz / 500 ml) milk
1 strip lemon zest
1 piece vanilla bean, 1 inch (3 cm) long
3 egg yolks
1/2 cup (4 oz / 125 g) sugar
1 tablespoon cornstarch
dash of salt
flavoring, to taste (armagnac, brandy, liqueur, or rum), optional

1. In a saucepan, bring the milk to boil with the lemon zest and vanilla bean over medium-high heat. Remove from heat and let cool. Remove vanilla bean and lemon zest.

2. In a bowl, combine the egg yolks, sugar, cornstarch, and salt. Beat with a whisk until pale yellow and the mixture forms ribbons when dropped from the whisk. Add some of the tepid milk, little by little, to the egg yolk mixture and stir well.

3. Stir the egg mixture into the remaining milk and place over medium-low heat. Cook very slowly for about ten minutes, stirring continually with a wooden spoon. The cream will start to thicken and should coat the spoon.

4. Remove from the heat and stir in flavoring, if desired. Pour into a bowl or container and stir from time to time as the custard cools.

Poplar tree plantation

Poached Pears
4 pears
1 bottle rosé wine
1/2 cup (4 oz/125 g) sugar
4 peppercorns
4 slivers fresh peeled ginger root

1. Peel the pears, leaving a cap of peel around the stem. Slice a thin layer off the bottom so they sit flat. Using a melon baller, core the pears from the bottom. They will be whole, intact, but hollow.

2. Place the rosé wine, sugar, peppercorns, and ginger root in a noncorrosive saucepan and bring to a boil over medium-high heat. Let boil until the liquid reduces a little and the wine cooks off some of its acidity, about five minutes.

3. Place the pears in the pan and reduce the heat to low. Cover and let poach for fifteen to twenty minutes or until the pears are soft when pierced with a fork.

4. Remove the pears from the pan and return the poaching liquid to a slow boil. Let reduce until you have a cup of sweet, pale pink wine syrup.

5. Place the pears on individual plates which have a lip or in shallow bowls. Drizzle the syrup over the pears and garnish with the following custard sauce flavored with two tablespoons of Poire William liqueur. Serve with a little ice-cold Poire William in a small brandy snifter or liqueur glass.

A Poet's Brandy

One summer day, Patrick and I were carrying out a little research and development across the hills that cradle the Garonne River Valley. We had been lunching in the jewel-like hill town Clermont-Dessous, which overlooks the long valley patched with fields of sunflowers and growing corn. The canal was just a slender shiny ribbon threaded through the many textures. With binoculars, I could see the *Julia Hoyt* and her giant white umbrella moored against the trout ponds at Bruch. She looked as small as a toy boat.

We spotted another hill town flanking Clermont-Dessous to the north. We jumped in the van and coasted down one steep slope then up another until we reached the crown at Bazens. This was a sleepy village, too. There were the ruins of an ancient château that lent evidence of a more active past. Mounted on the remaining château walls was a quote from Matteo Bandello. The Italian poet came here to seek company with the Italian nobles who were given the château by François I as a reward for their allegiance in battle. The inscribed brass plaque credits Matteo Bandello as the author of a tragic tale of two young lovers from quarrelling Italian families. This story was the basis for Shakespeare's "Romeo and Juliet" and residents of Bazen like to claim that the English have been coming here to steal poetic inspiration ever since.

Leaving the village and château behind, we descended through well-tended fruit orchards divided by low stone walls. I spotted a telltale invitation to another culinary adventure; a hand-lettered sign announcing *"Eau-de-vie de Poire William à vendre"* (Pear William brandy for sale). We parked beside the white linen laundry hanging in the sun and were greeted by the smiling round face of Monsieur Gros. This was his distillery, next to his old solid stone house where, together with his apple-cheeked wife, he invited us into the newly converted barn to explain his artisanal distillery.

Once a thriving commercial pear orchard, M. Gros' small but sweet juicy fruit grown on the hillsides of the Garonne Valley now failed to meet

European Union standards for larger fruit size. Naturally grown, with no irrigation like good wine grapes, his pears were more concentrated in flavor; delicious, plentiful, but not big enough. Without stopping to lament the politics or argue his position, he told us how he learned to distill the William pears prized in France for their sweet flavor. He found an old copper Cognac alambic (still) and installed it in the former milking shed of the barn. He macerated the fruit in shiny stainless steel tanks and then distilled the pulp and juice drop by drop. The crystal clear essence of pear, the eau-de-vie, is bottled in tall slender carafes with a portrait of Matteo Bandello, the patron poet of Bazens, on the label.

I spotted a squat round vat tucked to one side in the corner of the "brandy barn." "More Poire William?" I asked. Monsieur Gros straightened his work shirt, lowered his voice, and grinned. "That is my experiment," he confided. "Come. What do you smell?"

I timidly bent over the face-sized opening and nervously started to inhale the warm fumes. As the first gentle breath of perfumed vapors reached my nose, I opened my mouth and swallowed some of the moist air. "*C'est des fleurs!*" I exclaimed. "It's flowers," I translated to Patrick, who always lets me try things like this first. Monsieur Gros settled back down on the heels of his rubber farm shoes and rocked once for approval. "*Oui.* It's honeysuckle flowers distilled in my finest brandy." The artisanal distiller explained that the heavenly scented brandy would be gently sweetened with cane syrup to become a 74 proof liqueur called "*Saute Buissons*" and he proudly showed us the label on his first experimental bottle, a brightly colored drawing of the wildflowers. Monsieur Gros explained that although the French word for honeysuckle is *chèvrefeuille*, saute buissons (jump the hedgerows) is the old country name for wild honeysuckle. He slowly grinned once more as he said, "I think it's a little more...well, more Matteo Bandello." Everyone is a poet in my long village.

FRAISES AU VIN
Drunken Strawberries
Serves 4—6

From grand cafe menus to Mamie's simple kitchen, Garonne Valley strawberries are offered steeped, stewed, and soaked in wine. Simply delicious when made with the best ripe strawberries in June and a bottle of good, flavorful red wine, this is a refreshing summer dessert. Chilled and served in the wine, these soupy berries finish a Gascon meal on a high note, like eating summer in a bowl. Prepared in the morning, they will be perfect by dinner.

2 lb (1 kilo) very ripe strawberries, whole, stems removed
1 bottle hearty red wine
3 tablespoons sugar
1 cinnamon stick
zest of 1 orange
1/2 cup (4 fl oz/60 ml) armagnac or brandy

1. Place strawberries in a large bowl.
2. Pour the wine into a saucepan with the sugar, cinnamon stick, and zest and bring to a lively boil over medium-high heat. Let the mixture cook for five minutes.
3. When the wine has cooled some, add the armagnac or brandy, pour over the berries, and let them steep.
4. When the strawberries are cooled to room temperature, move them to the refrigerator and chill for several hours before serving.

CRÈME AU CITRON "BELLEVUE"
Lemon Cream "Bellevue"
Serves 4

More than the creamy calves and ripening cornfields, the strutting hens and polka-dotted guinea hens, the flamboyant Italian lemon tree burdened with dozens of fruit is the symbol of Bellevue, my neighbor's farm. Growing in a giant old wine barrel, the *citronnier* is a family affair; Grand-père Camille tends its care and grafts its new shoots onto hardy rootstock for neighbors,

Grand-mère Yvette fills the clever drip irrigation system (an old five-gallon plastic jug with a few holes poked in the bottom); *fils* Denis shovels a rich spadeful of compost from the barn into its tub from time to time, belle-fille Brigitte squeezes the juicy yellow fruit for fresh lemonade and creamy lemon puddings for the family. The sweet sharp fruit is shared generously with neighbors and friends. Like a postcard souvenir, the lemon tree,

framed by the big glass windows of its winter garage, is a reminder of the Italian heritage brought to France by Camille and his brothers.

3 eggs
2/3 cup (6 oz/180 g) sugar
1 tablespoon flour
juice of 2 lemons (Use only fresh lemons.)
1 teaspoon grated lemon zest
2 tablespoons butter
1 tablespoon rum

1. In a saucepan, combine the eggs, sugar, flour, lemon juice, and zest. Whisk furiously until a smooth sunflower-yellow cream is formed. Place over medium-low heat and stir continually with the whisk.

2. When the mixture starts to thicken, continue to beat, removing from heat from time to time so that you can really whip it up and control the cooking temperature.

3. Add the butter in two or three pieces and whisk after each piece. Lower the heat and continue to cook over low heat for three to five minutes or until the floury taste is gone.

4. Remove from heat and pour into a bowl. Whisk in the rum and let cool. Serve chilled or at room temperature. Pour into small bowls and serve with short-bread cookies or crispy wafers.

LA FERME BELLEVUE

The late afternoon sun escaping toward Biarritz sprays the lemon tree gold at the farm "Bellevue." Tractors are crawling in the background across fields of mown hay and the Sabadini's flock of chickens and pintades (guinea fowl) are parading fat thighs on the one-lane road. I visit the neighboring farm, ferme Bellevue, to stock the larder with more fresh goods and learn a new recipe or two. My visiting friends like to come along and stroke the golden forelocks of the gentle blonde cows as I pick out a couple of pintades for tomorrow's dinner.

Grand-mère Yvette of
La Ferme Bellevue

Bellevue sits up high on the corner overlooking the canal. The three-generation Sabadini family that lives and works on the well-stocked farm teaches me about farm husbandry, local folklore, and well-raised food. Tiny Grand-mère Yvette handles the rabbits and chooses a plump one for me, then does the hard work, preparing it for cooking. She's the one who taught me that you can't cook a freshly killed rabbit but must let it rest for a day; I didn't own a cookbook that could tell me that. Grand-père and grown son, Camille and Denis, tend to the herd of beautiful beef cattle, the Blondes of Aquitaine, that they raise. From the brawny bull, nose ring and all, to the cream-colored calves, the Blondes are a source of pride not just for ferme Bellevue, but for the entire département of the Lot-et-Garonne. In fields and near barns, I see these lean and muscular cattle as walking billboards for healthy country living.

Fruit is abundant in the Garonne Valley. The apples from our untended orchard, the fifty-foot-tall cherry tree across from the barn, the plum orchards all around the valleys, the wild chestnuts by the canal, and especially, the Italian lemon tree, white and yellow peach orchards, and fig trees at ferme Bellevue all contribute to the recipes and full pantries of the *Julia Hoyt* and in our farmhouse at Camont.

From picking strawberries to feeding the geese and ducks, the Sabadinis are generous with the time they share with us. An invitation to visit is an invitation to go back to the *Julia Hoyt* laden with fresh eggs for custards and creams, a guinea hen to bathe in armagnac and then roast, or, from the garden, some stalks of *vendengeurs* (harvesters), the little purple asters that flower during grape harvest time. Brigitte passes the word when someone has a spare freezer for sale or an old armoire that would be perfect in the new pigeonnier bedroom. Chrystelle and Bruno, the children, invite us to the village fêtes, local weddings, and Sunday dinner whenever we are free. The year I needed a suckling pig *and* the recipe for how to prepare it *and* thirty chairs to seat around three long tables, it was the busy farm at the top of the road that provided that, too. I once told friends looking to buy a house in the French countryside, "Forget the view, the old oak beams, the thickness of the walls, the lovely roses in the garden; it's the neighbors that count." Without all of the neighbors at Camont, the charm of old stones would swiftly fade.

CLAFOUTIS AUX PRUNEAUX
Custard-Cake with Prunes
Serves 4 — 6

Both custard and cake, this "eggy" dessert is a favorite in France, especially throughout the Gascon countryside. In the north of France, *clafoutis* is made with cherries in season, pears, or other fruit. But in Gascony, where succulent plums abound, the jam-like texture of slow-baked prunes steeped in armagnac adds a chewy richness to this homey dessert.

1 tablespoon butter
1/2 lb (250 g) soft pitted prunes
1/4 cup (2 fl oz/60 ml) armagnac or brandy (for a nonalcoholic substitute, use hot tea)
6 tablespoons flour
5 tablespoons sugar
5 eggs
3 cups (24 fl oz/750 ml) milk

1. Preheat the oven to 350 degrees F (175 C). Butter a shallow 1 1/2-quart (1 1/2-liter) baking dish and powder with sugar or flour.

2. Soak the prunes in the armagnac (or hot tea) at least thirty minutes or until they have absorbed most of the liquid. This can be done a day or more in advance.

3. In a large bowl, mix the flour and sugar. Beat the eggs in another bowl. Pour the beaten eggs into the flour and sugar and, with a whisk, add the milk little by little until all is well mixed.

4. Drain the prunes well and arrange in the pan in an even layer. Pour any leftover armagnac into the batter and mix. (If you have used hot tea, discard any leftover liquid.)

5. Pour the batter carefully around and over the prunes without disturbing them.

6. Bake for forty-five minutes or until a knife inserted in the center of the casserole comes out clean. Let cool completely and serve from the pan or unmold on a serving platter. This will be just as delicious served the next day as the aromatized prunes continue to perfume the "cake."

Variation

To make *millas*, a traditional cornmeal custard-cake of Gascony, substitute very fine ground cornmeal for half of the flour. (I regrind commercial cornmeal in a clean coffee mill to get the finer-textured corn "flour" available in France.)

FLAN AU FLOC ENCORE
Flanagan's Flan Again

Floc de Gascon is the Armagnac region's answer to Cognac's Pineau des Charentes and is a staple on the aperitif bar on the *Julia Hoyt* and in the summer garden at Camont. Everyone loves the smooth, nutty-sweet flavor of this Gascon aperitif. If you didn't bring back a bottle of Floc de Gascon from your last trip or can't find a bottle of Pineau des Charentes, substitute a nutty tasting sherry or Madeira for the flavoring.

2 cups (16 fl oz / 500 ml) milk
1 tablespoon orange zest
1 cinnamon stick
4 egg yolks
4 tablespoons sugar
1 teaspoon flour or cornstarch
1 jigger Floc de Gascon (or Pineau des Charentes, sherry, or Madeira)
1/4 cup toasted, crushed hazelnuts (filberts)

1. Preheat the oven to 325 degrees F (165 C).

2. Bring the milk, half of the orange zest, and cinnamon almost to a boil. Let them cool together and infuse the milk with the flavors.

3. Beat the egg yolks with the sugar and flour. Add a little of the tepid milk to the egg mixture and mix well. Pour the egg mixture and the floc into the milk and mix well.

4. Pour the flan mixture into small serving dishes, ramekins, or oven-proof bowls and place in a bain-marie in the oven. Bake for twenty-five to thirty minutes or until a knife plunged into the center of the flan comes out clean. Remove from oven and let cool. Serve room temperature or chilled. Garnish with a sprinkling of the crushed, toasted hazelnuts, and orange zest.

TOUR DE CRÊPES AU CHOCOLAT
Crêpes and Chocolate Tower
Serves 4—6

In the wine-producing village of Buzet, Madame Laffargue makes an impressive tower of armagnac-scented crêpes alternating with layers of rich crème pâtissière. The whole stack is covered with fluffy meringue and browned in a very hot oven like a baked Alaska. Sliced and served with a generous pool of crème anglaise on the side, this is always a favorite when we dine at her elegant restaurant, Le Vigneron. On the *Julia Hoyt*, I simplify the process and alternate the crêpes with crème pâtissière finished with just a shower of powdered sugar. Simpler still, the crew prefers it when I just grate dark bittersweet chocolate over each crepe as I stack the warm circles on top of each other. To finish, I simply grate more chocolate over the top and serve a bowl of thick crème fraîche alongside. I make the batter ahead of time and cook the crêpes as everyone is finishing their last course.

Armagnac, orange flower water, orange or lemon zest, rum, vanilla, and anise are some of the flavorings that go into the Gascon chef's parfum for crêpes and cakes. Each chef has their own "secret" formula, but a commercial version called *Crêp'arome* is available in country groceries. I recommend that you start with a tablespoon of flavoring and add more to your taste; plain sugared crêpes can take more flavoring.

2 cups (8 oz/250 g) sifted flour
1/2 cup (4 oz/125 g) sugar
pinch of salt
6 eggs
3 cups (24 fl oz/750 ml) milk
2 tablespoons melted butter
1 tablespoon flavoring
8 oz (250 g) dark chocolate

1. Place the flour, sugar, and salt in a bowl.
2. Crack the eggs in another bowl and beat lightly. Add the eggs to the flour and beat briskly with a whisk until smooth.

3. Add the milk, little by little, beating vigorously as you go. If needed, stir in some water to make a batter just thick enough to coat a wooden spoon and thin enough to pour easily.

4. Stir in the melted butter. Let the batter rest a couple of hours before cooking the crêpes.

5. After the batter has rested, add the flavoring. Prepare a crêpe pan or a small skillet by rubbing a little butter across the surface. Nonstick pans work well and need buttering only from time to time. Cook the crêpes and stack on a large serving plate, grating chocolate with a hand grater or hand-mill over each one as the next crêpe cooks. Build a tower twelve to twenty crêpes high and finish by grating more chocolate over the top. Serve by cutting into four to six wedges and passing a bowl of whipped crème fraîche or fresh cream around.

PETITS MONETS
Chocolate Butter Cream
Serves 4 to 6

When the *Julia Hoyt* moors under the poplar trees at Camont, the crew reminds me to reward their week-long diligence with one of their favorite desserts! We dubbed this classic chocolate cream *Petits Monets*; a tribute to a recipe described in Monet's kitchen journals. Since the version I make for crew and guests is so rich that just a spoonful or two is needed, we competed to invent different ways to serve the decadent *crème chocolat*. My favorite is the most literal, just a spoonful!

4 oz (125 g) sweet dark chocolate
2 tablespoons soft unsalted butter
2 eggs
1 dash orange flower water or other flavoring
1/2 cup (4 fl oz/125 ml) crème fraîche

1. Heat the chocolate over a very low flame or in a double boiler until it just melts. Add the butter bit by bit to the warm chocolate and stir with a whisk until the mixture is very smooth.

2. Add the eggs, one at a time, to the chocolate mixture, beating briskly after each egg. As the cream starts to thicken, remove the pan from the heat.

3. Add a dash of orange flower water and stir. Let cool.

4. When the chocolate mixture is at room temperature, swirl in the crème fraîche. Pour the chocolate cream into four individual pots, ramekins, or pretty egg cups. The smaller the serving the better, as this is a very rich dessert. Refrigerate or let sit in a cool place until ready to serve. Top with a dab of crème fraîche on each pot. Another way to serve is to pour the mixture into a small bowl and chill. Place six large silver soup spoons in the freezer. When ready to serve, take a frozen spoon and scoop a big round of firm chocolate cream onto it. Place on a pretty saucer and serve with a couple of lacy wafers and a cup of strong coffee or glass of armagnac.

FROMAGE EN DOUCE
Goat Cheese with Armagnac and Honey

I first tasted this subtly honeyed goat cheese at La Belle Gasconne in Poudenas. Characteristic of the thoughtful elegance of the Soubiran-Gracia kitchen, the cheese course of the *dégustation* ("tasting") menu featured just two perfect cheeses; a nutty wedge of aged cheese from the Pyrenees, and a spoonful of very fresh goat cheese that was sweetened, flavored with armagnac, and served with a slice of homemade prune-walnut bread. I often serve this dessert-cheese course to finish a meal on the *Julia Hoyt* with flourish. The clean tastes of country honey and creamy fresh goat cheese are enhanced by the flavorful Gascon armagnac.

8 oz (250 g) fresh mild-flavored goat cheese
1 tablespoon armagnac
1 tablespoon honey

1. Soften the goat cheese by hand in a bowl.

2. Stir the armagnac and honey into the softened cheese. Taste and correct, if necessary, by adding more honey or brandy to your liking. Let sit at room temperature for an hour to marry the flavors. Serve with slices of prune-walnut or other fruit-nut bread.

Note: In French, *douce* means sweet and *en douce* means "on the sly." This is "cheese on the sly"—cheese masquerading as dessert.

A Hearthside Feast

When the busy season is over and August descends like a nap, "the friends" arrive. The year that our good friend Franny arrived, travel-stained from three years in Turkey, was the first year of inaugurating the kitchen with its large open hearth, or cheminée, at Camont.

I was eager for the first cool evenings so that I could build a cozy fire and cook a whole dinner over the coals. I had found rusty grills and an old iron crémaillère hook on which to hang a copper kettle. A set of antique andirons was presented to us by neighbors, and pokers and tools were collecting in a corner. But when Franny, the artist, arrived with her bright paintings of minarets and Turkish markets and a housewarming present of a dozen ornate skewers, I knew the time was right. I went to the poultry market in Agen and asked the *marchande de volaille* (poultry vendor) to save me two demoiselles, or young ladies, the Gascon name for a duck carcass. The foie gras, the magret, legs for confit, and all other important parts had been sold separately. What remains is the tasty meat clinging to the ribs, similar to spareribs. I bought a round *boule* of yeasty bread, a kilo of rough-skinned baking potatoes, and a bottle of deep red wine.

I built a small cooking fire, stick by stick, like some African women had taught me years ago in Zaire, using branches of a walnut tree that was felled by lightning and old age. I fed the fire branch by branch until I had a thick bed of coals. Franny gathered some of the small apples that still drop acid-sweet from the long-ignored orchard and threaded them on the brass-handled skewers as she regaled me with stories of Istanbul and Turkish food markets.

The potatoes were wrapped in heavy aluminum foil and put into the coals to one side of the cheminée. They would take the longest to cook. As they started, I chopped a persillade (garlic and parsley garnish) and cut the duck carcasses in two. The apples were put over the cooler coals on a grill to bake slowly, their natural juices caramelizing as they cooked, and the bottle of hearty local wine was opened and poured. Alternating dark prunes and spicy sausages on the skewers, we toasted *brochettes d'Agen* and ate them as hot aperitif morsels.

I placed the duck ribs with all their succulent meat attached over the hottest part of the fire and we pulled the metal garden chairs closer to the heat. The evening was cooling off and a light autumn wind carried the smoke out of the chimney across the canal just as it did one hundred years ago, the last time someone lived in this house. Franny and I watched the demoiselles turn a crispy brown as the marrow juices started to hiss and vaporize in the heat.

I had a big covered casserole dish ready and, when the meat was cooked to medium-rare, we placed the carcasses in the pan, sprinkled the meat and bones with the persillade, and placed the cover on it so the meat would steep in the garlicky bits on the edge of the wide fireplace. The potatoes were retrieved from the ashes and we broke them open over bowls and ground a generous shower of fresh salt and pepper over the steaming potato flesh. We tied antique linen towels monogrammed with old-fashioned initials around our necks and tucked into the "young ladies," juice running down our chins. The aiguillette, the tenderloin that lies along the bone and near the prized liver, is the tastiest bit. What a menu!

Pulling closer to the fire to reheat a bit of the carcass crispier over the fire, we toasted poor Jeanne d'Arc, another demoiselle toasted on the flames. The roasted apples fell off the skewers into our mouths, burning our impatient tongues. Sweet with natural sugars, the juices exploded through the smooth skins and dripped in caramel stripings. I sweetened a little fresh goat's cheese with honey and armagnac, to complement the hot apples. This was the first dinner cooked in Camont's old kitchen in over one hundred years and it's also one of my all-time favorite meals. When autumn rolls around each year, I start to gather branches.

Menu
Brochettes d'Agen (Prune and Sausage
    Brochettes)
Demoiselles Grillées (Grilled Duck
    Carcasses)
Patates aux Cindres (Potatoes Cooked in
    the Ashes)
Pommes Rôties (Roasted Fallen Apples)
    and Fromage en Douce (Cheese on
    the Sly)

Ingredients List

AILLETS: Young garlic shoots, called "green garlic," harvested in the early spring, are steamed and sautéed, or used to add a subtle garlic flavor to dishes.

ARMAGNAC: The distinctive regional brandy made in the Armagnac region of Southwest France. Although cognac or other brandies can be substituted, they won't contribute the complex flavor of Gascony's armagnac.

BOUQUET GARNI: A small bundle of fresh herbs such as thyme, parsley, and bay leaf, often tied with a string or placed in a cheesecloth pouch and used to flavor soups and stews.

BROUTES: Young tender cabbage shoots available in the fall. Tender collard greens, kale, and beet greens can be substituted.

CONFIT: The preserved meat specialty of Southwest France; usually refers to pork, goose, or duck. Confit de canard (preserved duck) and confit d'oie (preserved goose) are available in glass jars, aluminum cans, or vacuum packed in plastic pouches. The meat has been salt-cured then slow-cooked in its own fat, and is of a particularly tender and silky texture. The nut-like flavor of confits permeates regional dishes like garbure and can be made at home or purchased from specialty sources (see Source List).

CORNICHONS: Tiny, vinegared pickles (gherkins) often accompanying pâtés, terrines, sausages, and other meats.

CRÈME FRAÎCHE: A cultured, heavy cream that thickens and develops a delicate tangy taste as it ages. Crème fraîche is available in some dairy sections around the U.S., but its easy enough to make at home. The thick cultured cream is used instead of heavy cream to add body and richness to sauces and gratin dishes since it doesn't break down under high heat. A dollop of crème fraîche provides a subtle counterpoint to sweet desserts. Try spooning some of it over fruit desserts and fresh berries. To make a simple crème fraîche, combine one cup (8 oz/250 ml) of heavy cream and two tablespoons of active culture buttermilk in a clean jar. Cover and leave at room temperature (an unlit oven is a good place) twelve hours, or until thickened. Refrigerate and use as needed. The tart flavor will continue to develop over time. Crème fraîche will keep one to two weeks or longer in the refrigerator.

DUCK AND GOOSE FAT: Duck and goose fat are the most commonly used cooking oils in Southwest France. Indeed, the use of these fats defines Gascony more than any geographical boundary. The subtle flavor of the pure, rendered fat is a key ingredient in the character of Gascon cuisine. Duck fat is available from foie gras producers (see Source List) and lasts several weeks in the refrigerator. Substitute any high-quality cooking oil (sunflower, corn, peanut, olive oils) for duck fat or use unsalted butter in recipes not calling for high cooking temperatures.

EAU-DE-VIE: Brandy, distilled either from fruit or wine, is drunk as a *digestive* (after-dinner drink) or used to fortify flavored aperitif wine. Armagnac and cognac are eaux-de-vie de vin (brandies made from wine) particular to the regions for which they are named. Poire William, mirabelle, and framboise are common fruit eaux-de-vie made from pears, plums, and raspberries.

FOIE GRAS: The liver of a duck or goose fattened by force feeding, literally the "fat liver." Similar to corn feeding cattle in feedlots before butchering, the gavage (force feeding) of ducks produces a tender, tasty meat as well as the healthy, but large, liver. Foie gras is available fresh (uncooked) or in tins or jars fully cooked, domestic and imported. The best foie gras has a light creamy color, buttery texture, and mild taste.

GARLIC: Like all other produce, garlic has a limited shelf life; the bulb will sprout, dry out, or rot eventually. Keep fresh garlic in a cool, airy, and dark area (I use a covered basket) and buy fresh garlic frequently. Always remove the bitter green germ from the middle of the clove.

HERBS: Fresh herbs are referred to in most recipes and I like their texture as well as their "liveliness." Herbs are easy to grow, both in pots or in gardens, and fresh parsley, thyme, basil, rosemary, sage, and chives are now available in supermarket produce sections. Dried bay leaves are easily available but make sure, as with all dried herbs, that they still have some of their essence. (The jar of dried sage you bought five years ago for the Christmas turkey might need to be replaced.) You can substitute dried herbs for fresh but remember to adjust the quantity as dried herbs are more potent per measurement.

MUSHROOMS: *Cèpes* (Boletus edulis) is the favored wild mushroom of Southwest France. Other tasty choices available are *trompettes de la mort* (poor man's truffles), *chanterelles, pleurotes, girolles,* and morels. Canned and dried mushrooms of these varieties are available and can be combined with fresh domestic mushrooms.

OILS: Sunflower, corn, peanut, and grapeseed oils are the common cooking and salad oils in Southwest France when neutrality is called for. Duck and goose fat are used for adding flavor to cooking and olive oil is used sparingly in salads since its distinctive flavor distracts the Southwest palate. Walnut and hazelnut oils are wonderful when used in dressings and on vegetables.

ORANGE FLOWER WATER: One of the key ingredients for flavorings crêpes, sweets, and cakes, pure orange flower water, distilled from orange flowers, is available imported from France. Mix with armagnac, lemon zest, anise essence (or pastis), vanilla, and rum for a Gascon-style flavoring.

PAIN DE CAMPAGNE: Literally "country bread," this hearty bread is used in stuffings and for serving with soups, as croutons or toasts. The heavy-textured bread stands up to liquids and is the basis for crusty, garlicky toasts.

PERSILLADE: The final touch to many Gascon dishes, a persillade is simply a big bunch of parsley chopped finely with a few cloves of garlic. Sprinkled generously over cooked meats, fowl, and potaotes, it serves as a fresh seasoning to the finished dish.

POULE AND POULET: The first is a stewing hen, the second is a fryer. To confuse them is to court culinary disaster: a tough, inedible bird improperly cooked or a tasteless, overdone chicken mush.

POULTRY: The chickens, ducks, and guinea hens called for in these simple recipes must be the best farm-raised poultry that you can find. The corn-fed free-range farm poultry free of hormone injections and other additives is the basis for this healthy and hearty cuisine. In France, a farm-raised fowl costs twice what its commercial supermarket cousin costs. Guinea hens, ducklings, and other game are available from mail-order sources (see Source List). It's worth the effort to find an old-fashioned butcher shop that can secure high-quality meats and poultry for you.

PRUNES: The succulent and sweet slow-baked plums found in France are unlike the overdried, sulphured prunes Americans think of as medicine. Prunes are a delicacy as valued as rich chocolates and jewel-like *fruits glacés* (candied fruit). Used in many recipes of Southwest France, they contribute a sweet and rich flavor either on their own or steeped in armagnac, wine, or eau-de-vie. I have found that the best prunes available come in cans and especially recommend those organically grown and preserved. (See Source List.)

QUATRE ÉPICES: Special to the Southwest, "four spices" usually contains five—pepper, cloves, nutmeg, ginger, and cinnamon. I make this mixture as I need it by grinding the whole spices in a mortar and pestle or in a small electric mill or coffee grinder. The freshly ground spices are more pungent.

SEA SALT: The flavor of salt changes from area to area and sea salt is especially different from mined salt. The hand-harvested "gray salts" of the Atlantic coast, from the Île de Ré and Brittany, are noted for their distinctive seaweed influence and are graded and awarded under French law. Less salt is needed, since the flavor is more concentrated, and I tend to salt lightly but at the end of cooking preparation.

VANILLA SUGAR: I like to buy the little French packets of *sucre vanille* found in the supermarkets and *épiceries* for their pretty envelopes engraved with sailing ships and fin-de-siècle lettering. Otherwise simply place one or two vanilla bean pods in a jar, fill the jar with sugar, and seal. Store in your pantry cupboard until needed and replenish with more sugar as needed.

VANILLA VINEGAR: Although it is available in some specialty stores, vanilla vinegar is just as easy to make. Place a fresh vanilla bean or two in a long narrow jar and cover with good white wine vinegar or champagne vinegar. Let infuse for a week or longer, then use on fruit, salad dressings, or to enliven melon soup.

VEGETABLES: Fennel, celery root, eggplants (aubergines), zucchini (courgettes), leeks, and endive are common garden vegetables available in most produce departments.

VENTRECHE: This rolled, salted, peppery pork belly is used to flavor many cooked dishes, vegetable or meat. Italian pancetta (a close relative), salt pork, or a fatty piece of unsmoked ham or bacon can be substituted for *ventreche* in cooking. A thick slice chopped into rough cubes is "worked" in the hot pan with a little duck fat. This rich flavor permeates the slow-cooked cabbage, potatoes, and stews.

VERVEINE: Also called lemon verbena, this wonderful herb is used to perfume flans, custards, and teas. Easily available as dried loose leaf in health food stores or packaged as an herbal tea. Homemade eaux-de-vie are also flavored with verveine.

VINEGARS: Red wine vinegar made from homemade wines is commonly used in Southwest France and adds one more rustic element to the cuisine. Varying in degree of acidity and strength, vinegars, if well balanced, can add a distinctive touch to country sauces and soups. Homemade wine vinegar can be started with a "mother," aged in a wooden cask or ceramic pot, and added to from time to time with leftover wine. Taste several brands of wine vinegars to find a flavorful and balanced vinegar for your vinaigrettes and cooking.

WINES: Some of the regional wines of Southwest France besides those from the Bordeaux *appellation* include: Bergerac, Cahors, Côtes de Buzet, Côtes de Bruilhois, Côtes de Duras, Côtes de Frontonnais, Côtes de Marmandais, Côtes de St. Mont, Gaillac, Jurancon, Madiran, Pacherenc du Vic Bilh, and Tursan.

GLOSSARY

ARTISANAL: The craftsman-like and individual approach to various disciplines; *artisanal charcutier* (pork butcher), *artisanal boulanger* (bread baker), *artisanal distillerie* (distillery).

AUBERGE: Inn or restaurant.

BARQUE: Small boat or barge.

BATELIER: Boatman or bargee.

BOUDIN: Black pudding or blood sausage.

BOULE: A round loaf of country-style bread.

BOULES: The popular game played with steel balls, also called Petanque in the Southwest.

CHARCUTERIE: The pork-butcher shop and its products, including fresh pork, sausages, boudins, pâtés, and cured hams and meat. A sort of delicatessen.

CHEMINÉE: The hearth and fireplace; the focus of the rustic kitchen.

CIVET: A red wine-based slow-cooking stew for game or poultry.

CONFIT: Although used here most frequently to refer to preserved duck and goose, *confit de canard* and *confit d'oie*, the term can also mean candied fruits.

CONFITURES: From the verb *confire* meaning to pickle, to preserve, to candy, and to pot. Confitures are the products of these methods and usually refer to jams.

CRÉMAILLÈRE: The long iron hook from which pots are suspended over the fire in a *cheminée*.

CRÊPES: Thin griddle cakes made with eggs, flour, and milk and usually served as dessert. Savory-filled crêpes are called *galettes*, and are usually made with buckwheat flour.

DEMOISELLE: Literally meaning young lady, *demoiselle* refers to the carcass of a duck.

DÉPARTEMENT: The term for a province, or state, in France.

ÉCLUSE: A lock or lock-gate used to lower or raise the water level of a canal.

ÉPICERIE: A small grocery store with a variety of goods.

FARCI: A stuffing made from bread, meats, or other ingredients for vegetables, meats, and poultry.

FERME: A farm.

FERME AUBERGE: A working farm that receives visitors for food and/or accommodations.

FÊTE: The village festival or celebration, as in the Fête du Canal.

FRANC: The French money unit that is divided into centimes (hundredths).

GARBURE: The famous cabbage, bean, and confit stew of Gascony.

GIRONDE: The name of both the estuary and the département in which the Garonne River meets the Atlantic Ocean past Bordeaux.

LOT-ET-GARONNE DÉPARTEMENT: The governmental province that includes both the Garonne and Lot rivers. Agen is the capital of this département.

MARCHAND DE VOLAILLE: Poultry merchant or market vendor.

MISTRAL: The strong north wind that descends on the Rhône Valley.

PARFUM: In culinary terms parfum, referring to flavor rather than scent, is of course about both.

PASTIS: The anise-flavored sweet aperitif popular throughout France.

PÂTE: Pastry, dough, paste, or pasta, not to be confused with *pâté*.

PÂTÉ: Meat or vegetable loaf cooked and served fresh or preserved in jars.

PAYSAN AND PAYSANNE: Countryman and countrywoman, the laborers, fieldworkers, and peasants.

PÉNICHE: Barge or canal-boat.

PIGEONNIER: Dovecote or pigeon tower built to house and protect pigeons.

POISSONNERIE: Fishmonger.

PRUNE: Fresh plum.

PRUNEAUX: Dried plums.

RELAIS: An inn formerly used as a posting stop or stage on a traveler's route.

SABOTS: Wooden shoes.

TAPENADE: An olive and anchovy paste.

TARTE: A filled pastry crust pie.

TERRINE: An earthenware baking pan or a pâté baked in one.

TOURTE: Thin pastry-covered savory pie served as an entrée or aperitif.

Source List

Foie gras, duck fat, and specialty poultry products are available at some gourmet shops and specialty stores around the country. Mail-order is an easy alternative from two reputable companies with informative catalogues.

D'Artagnan
399 Saint Paul Avenue
Jersey City, NJ 07306
Telephone (800) DARTAGNAN or (201) 792-0748

Sonoma Foie Gras
P.O.Box 2007
Sonoma, CA 95476
Telephone (800) 427-4559 or (707) 938-1229

Prunes. The best prunes that I've found in America come from a Sonoma County producer, Timber Crest Farms. The flavorful French-style prunes are packaged in cans and available directly from the farm's retail store or at gourmet food shops around the country. For more information contact:

Timber Crest Farms
4791 Dry Creek Road
Healdsburg, CA 95448
Telephone (707) 433-8251

The Julia Hoyt

The *Julia Hoyt* is available for private four-passenger luxury charters along the Canal Latéral à la Garonne in Southwest France. In addition to these canal cruises, author Kate Ratliffe also offers week-long cooking adventures in the country kitchens of Gascony. For more information about *Julia Hoyt* Canal Cruises and European Culinary Adventures, contact:

Kate Ratliffe
P.O. Box 888
Mendocino, CA 95460
(800) 852-2625
(508) 535-5738

INDEX

Index

INDEX

ACKNOWLEDGMENTS

In France, I must first thank Christian Barthe, barge builder, who was the first to welcome me and the *Julia Hoyt* to Agen. Claude and Vetou Pompèle, Yannick, Melinda, and Clotilde-Julia have unconditionally shared their table and lives with me and the many friends, family members, and clients whom I have invited. In the kitchen, Vetou never hesitated to share her secrets and encourage me to write them down.

The Famille Sabadini opened the doors of their working farm, Bellevue, to me and taught me about my clucking, mooing, and quacking Gascon neighbors. Monsieur and Madame Dupuy kept the old Gascon patois alive, telling me stories of fêtes and feasts over their seventy-plus years at Camont. Monique and Serge Madotta translated the old ways into a modern context for me.

Maria-Claude Gracia not only offered me authentic Gascon recipes from her beautiful *auberge*, La Belle Gasconne, but shared her *cuisine de passion* in a spirit of kinship, as Richard Gracia elevated the rigors of daily business to the heights of hospitality. Chefs Andre Daguin in Auch and Michel Guerard in Eugenie-le-Bains maintain their vision of the regional rustic cuisine in their elegant restaurants and unerringly share it with typical Gascon generosity. I thank Maïte and Micheline of *La Cuisine des Mousquetaires—France 3 Aquitaine* for putting poetry and laughter into their recounting of traditional dishes, and I especial[...] for *The Cooking of South-West France*, which gave me an English-language key to unde[...] ing, hearing, and tasting.

The community of barge families at Castets-en-Dorthe, especially Victor and Yvo[...] this tightly closed community to an American captain eager to hear stories of big boats [...] Tim and Lin Eliot of the *Mark Twain* always offered a generous and sympathetic Englis[...]

Along the way, friends became willing crews and willing crews became lifelong frie[...] always there when I needed a friend, galley slave, traveling partner, or critical eye. Ann[...] a captain in every sense of the word, from sails to souls. Kimberly and Tom Flanagan ke[...] true. Angel Stephen Eastman put the wind in my sails by never doubting that I could d[...] boat. Jhon, Rhonda, Jay, Lynda, Caroline, Kathy, Tomm, Valerie, and Franny crewed to[...] the leftovers, did the dishes, and lit the Chinese lanterns.

I thank the Hill family for their part in my becoming a barge queen: my sister, St[...] ries about Gascony twenty years ago, my brother and *belle-soeur*, Jeff and Ann, who ke[...] haven and homeport always open, and especially my mother, Phyllis, for keeping Juli[...] European Culinary Adventures functioning while I change time zones and schedules [...] my husband, Patrick, kept me on course as I insisted on living this fantasy. His patien[...] graciousness, and solid presence are my life anchor.

This book, too, was just another fantasy adventure until Cindy Frank and Sal G[...] me write it down. My Mendocino mentor, Camille Ranker, insisted on strength and [...] Press, Phil Wood took a chance on a canal cruise, and Kirsty Melville adopted my "[...] editor and guide, not only taught me the publishing ropes but allowed me to shape the [...] keep the duck fat in the recipes. John Miller at Big Fish Books took my photographs and words as if he'd found them in an old stone house by the side of the canal and created my *souvenir* journal; Jonathan Chester took honest recipe photos and shared adventure stories as we ate the delicious evidence. Finally, many thanks to the recipe-testing crew for their faith and culinary imagination: Phyllis, Jeff, Ann, Mike, Alvin, Renee, Annie, Kimberly, Tom, Rachelle, and Randy. Thank you all.